THE
TITHE

THE DOCTRINE
THAT IS HINDERING
THE CHURCH

WHY THE 10 COMMANDMENTS ARE NOT FOR BELIEVERS

BY
ALAN J. WINKLER

Dedication

It is difficult to imagine how this book would have come into being without the support of my wife, Vicki. She and I have been together for nearly twenty-five years, and throughout that time she has been the epitome of the Biblical definition of help-mate. Her support of me—while writing this book and getting the thoughts and pictures that have been in my head down on paper—has been everything I could have asked for.

Although it has been said many times, the old saying bears repeating to all who would read this book: behind anything a man accomplishes in this world, there typically stands a wife who supports, sustains, and sacrifices for his vision and efforts. A wife who rarely gets, or desires, any credit. This is especially true for me, and my wife, Vicki Winkler. Thank you for sticking around!

Table of Contents

Introduction

Have you ever been confused during a sermon from the pulpit of your church by contradictory statements? Perhaps you heard your pastor teach that the Old Covenant Mosaic Law was fulfilled by Jesus, and we are now saved by grace, then later in the service heard him say during the offertory that he would now receive your tithes. He may also have preached entire sermons as to why you should tithe. He may have gone even further and preached to you that if you are not tithing, you are robbing God and you will not be blessed.

If you have studied the Bible, you may think, *Wait a minute! Aren't these the same tithes that are part of the Old Covenant Mosaic Law that the pastor just preached has been fulfilled by Jesus?*

Your confusion is understandable as you progressively consider several facts:

1

1) We are saved by grace.

2) The Old Covenant Mosaic Law has been fulfilled by Jesus.

3) Tithing is part of the Old Covenant Mosaic Law that has been fulfilled.

4) Pastor is now asking me to tithe.

Your logic leads you to this concluding question: Why am I being asked to tithe, when the covenant that tithing is a part of is no longer in force?

If you have asked this question—or similar ones regarding giving—and are searching for truth from the Bible regarding giving and not men's opinions, you are not alone, and this book is for you. In fact, as the title The Tithe: The Doctrine That Is Hindering The Church suggests, once you understand true New Covenant giving, you will see that tithing—part of the Old Covenant Mosaic Law doctrine that Jesus fulfilled—is actually hindering the Body of Christ. How can this be? Old Covenant tithing is hindering the church because Jesus has fulfilled the Mosaic Law, He has given us a new one, and He is the mediator of a better covenant (Hebrews 8:6).

Leaders in the Body of Christ today seem intimidated by the idea that the doctrine of tithing is hindering the church, thinking, *If we teach the Body of Christ to stop tithing, won't they stop giving?* No, pastors, do not fear! Once the Body of Christ understands **grace giving**, then giving by the Body of Christ will increase in every assembly worldwide. True New Covenant giving is by grace (2 Corinthians 8:1-7)!

In the covenant that Believers live in today, Old Covenant tithing has been replaced by New Covenant grace giving directed by the Holy Spirit. As you read this book, you will discover that Jesus' Grace Covenant doesn't merely surpass the Mosaic Law Covenant in its power to save. Jesus' Grace Covenant, which includes how He wants us to give, also surpasses the Mosaic Law Covenant in its ability to bless both giver and receiver.

In this book, I take a non-religious, but Scriptural approach to the doctrine of tithing. Not only do I explain why tithing is not for the New Covenant, but I also bring to light the little-known fact that even under the Mosaic Law, God actually designated the majority of the tithes to be given to a group other than the Levites and priests.

Later, I will also address another argument pastors and teachers make regarding Abram and his giving a one-time tenth of his spoils to Melchizedek. I will show you that what Abram did before he was formally in covenant with God is not a teaching on tithing for the New Covenant at all. On the contrary, we will see that Abram's one-time offering is actually a prophetic picture of Jesus and the New Covenant.

After spending ten years diligently trying to follow the Mosaic Law as a Christian, I saw the fruitlessness of my efforts in mixing the two Covenants of Law and Grace. I subsequently received the teaching and revelation of grace alone for all things: the true Gospel of Jesus. This included learning who the tithes were for under the Mosaic Law, why tithing is not part of the New Covenant, and why the Mosaic Law is powerless to impact any part of Believer's lives.

I have written a book that is designed to give you a fresh perspective on not only giving, but also the juxtaposition of the Mosaic Law verses God's Grace for the New Covenant Believer. So, not only will we discuss tithing, but more broadly show that the entirety of the Old Covenant has been completely fulfilled by Jesus, for the Believer.

After reading this book, it is my hope that you will have been set free from any religious legalism regarding giving. Then, because of this, rather than giving based on the direction of an invalid, Old Covenant doctrine or teaching of man, you will be free to give what the Holy Spirit directs you to give. You will be free to serve God and the Holy Spirit in you, without the bondage of religion. Jesus did not come to bring religion, a word whose etymology is from the Latin words *re* (a prefix meaning "return") and *ligare* (which means "to bind"). So, the root of the word "religion" literally means **to return to bondage**. You will learn that both salvation and sanctification (our daily walk) are by grace alone.

The grace and peace of Jesus be with you.

Chapter One
The Covenants: The Choice is Yours

Despite what you may think because of the title, this is NOT a book that is advocating restraint in giving to the church. On the contrary, I believe in giving and in the promised results of giving.

Luke 6:38 – *"Give, and it will be given to you: good measure, pressed down, shaken together, and running over, will be given to you. For with the same measure you measure it will be measured back to you"* (World English Bible).

This book was written to set you free to obey the voice of God, the Holy Spirit in you. It seeks to encourage Believers to study and understand the differences between the Old Covenant and the New Covenant at their foundations, then their differences, specifically regarding giving. There is a stark difference in these two covenants: one is based on man's performance and is ineffective, and the other is based on Jesus, and better promises, and is effective. The question posed by this book is, "If we are trusting Jesus and His grace for salvation, power over sin and the devil, and healing, why are we trusting in the Mosaic Law for our giving?

Further, we will look at pictures in the Scriptures showing that the Old Covenant has been completely done away with for the Believer, including the Ten Commandments. Now, if that sounds like heresy, stick with me because I am not saying that the holiness of the Father in Heaven, has been done away with. However, I am saying that the means to living that holiness has changed—and that truly is Good News.

First, however, I'd like to share a little backstory with you regarding why I've written this book. My wife, Vicki, and I tried to live under the Mosaic Law, the Torah, for TEN years, and let me just say it now, "OUCH!" **It made us absolutely miserable!** Yet, it was originally given to the Hebrew nation. So, how does a Bible-believing couple, like us, get sidetracked into following the Torah?

To be honest, we had a sincere desire to please God, and at the time, we were studying the Hebrew roots of the Christian faith, the Feasts of Israel, Passover, Shavuot (now known as Pentecost) etc. As we studied, we saw Scriptures in the Old Covenant that said that the Hebrew Feasts (*moedim* in Hebrew), some of the most important parts of the Mosaic Law, were perpetual (Leviticus 23:41). If this was the case, then it made sense that the lesser items of the 613 ordinances of the Mosaic Law must also be part of our lifestyle.

Our mindset was, *Okay, we have been saved by the blood of Jesus and now this is how we are to live our lives on Earth. After all, we now have the Holy Spirit, so we have the power to do so, right?* Wrong! In our fervor, what we did not realize was how insidiously and subtly the bondage of the Mosaic Law would permeate our lives.

Another hallmark of attempting to follow the Mosaic Law is that it gives birth to its offspring: legalism. Everything had to be done perfectly and in a certain way. We also observed that there were vehement disagreements over seemingly trivial points among people who were trying to follow the Mosaic Law of the Sinai Covenant. There were many exhausting discussions, and a lot of stress, because we all wanted to get it right, so we could please God.

We had discussions about which day was the "real" Sabbath, or when was the "real" New Moon (i.e. was it the dark moon or the first sliver of the moon?). Should you wear a Tallit, the Hebrew prayer shawl, only during the Feasts or also at other times? On and on, it went! However, the most telling observation was that, by and large, most of these people were not what I would describe as happy people. In fact, many of them were quite angry. Sooner or later, as a Believer, you have to ask, "Where is the joy of the Lord?"

At the end of the day, our wake-up call was when we realized that all of what we were doing—and we were doing a lot of doing—was all about **us** instead of our Savior, **Jesus**. It is hard to fix your eyes upon Jesus, the author and finisher of your faith, and trust Him and His grace, when you are always looking at yourself and your behavior. This is a general truth about any area of your life: when all your focus is on yourself, you are going to be miserable.

As the sons of God (Galatians 4:6), this is not to be our purpose in life. We are to have our focus outward, not inward. This should also act as a red flag regarding which covenant you are operating under, since many people mix both the Mosaic Law and Jesus' grace together, without realizing it.

For instance, if you are mainly focused on your behavior and are very sin conscious, or worried about losing your salvation, there is a good chance that you are living under the Mosaic Law (or its offspring, legalism) instead of the grace of Jesus. The way of grace, the way of Jesus, is that the way you change your fruit— your behavior—is by changing your root—your spirit. Grace changes you by the power of the Holy Spirit from the inside out; the Mosaic Law can only try to change you by your own power, from the outside in. This is simply *how* these covenants were designed.

In other words, it is not just behavior modification; anyone can do that for a while by their own efforts. True, lasting change must occur at the spirit level through Jesus' gift of salvation. For

Vicki and me, it was not until we heard Joseph Prince teach on grace that we were able to see that we were really living in bondage to the Mosaic Law and legalism. He taught that we were already pleasing to God, our Father, just because of our position in God's family, in Jesus.

From that point forward, after receiving the word of grace, the true Gospel, we saw that our obedience to God was in trusting Jesus, His grace, and what He had done, not in ourselves. Any holiness in our walk on Earth would be by His grace, not our carnal efforts.

The Foundation

The initial task, before we discuss anything about tithing, is to show through Scripture that the Mosaic Law, in its entirety (including the Ten Commandments), has been done away with for the Believer, by Jesus. This is important, because if any part of the Mosaic Law is still in force for the Believer, then Yeshua (Jesus' Hebrew name) died for nothing! Therefore, the argument could be made that tithing should still be part of the message that we hear from our pulpits today. If we see and understand the difference at the foundational level, then all of what comes after it is more easily understood.

The Torah, or Mosaic Law, was established by YHVH, the Heavenly Father, through Moses for the Hebrew people, as His standard of holiness and righteousness for the world to see. Because of Israel's strategic location between Africa and Asia, a large percentage of the ancient world would get to see how blessed this tiny nation was and ask about their God. What gets lost to us in the western world, is that the Old Covenant Law was much more than just the Ten Commandments. It was a performance based, conditional covenant of **613 Laws** that the **Hebrews**, the Father's Old Covenant people, were to perform to attain righteousness and maintain relationship with Him.

The Name

Before I go any further, for clarity's sake, let me address the use of the four letters representing the Father's personal name that I have used above. **Y-H-V-H** (in Hebrew: yud, hey, vav, hey) are the four letters that represent the Father's actual name. It was traditionally written **Yahweh** and pronounced "YAH-way."

In Hebrew, each letter of the alphabet has a corresponding number. The first letter, *Aleph*, is assigned the number one, the second letter, *Bet* is assigned the number two, and so on. Additionally, there are pictures that are assigned to each of the letters.

It is an amazing fact that if you look at the corresponding pictures of the four letters of God's personal name, you will see JESUS. What do I mean? The picture for *Yud* is a **hand**, the picture for *Hey* is man with arms raised, or looking out a window, and it means **grace**. The picture for *Vav* is a **nail**, and the final letter of God's personal name is another *Hey*, or more **grace.** To construct a sentence of the four letters of God's name, you would say, **"The hand of grace nailed in more grace."** Jesus was nailed to a cross and is the mediator of the *grace covenant.* Jesus is God!

YHVH is also known as the Tetragrammaton. In fact, according to many Jewish sources, the original Hebrew of the Bible did not have vowels or punctuation, nor spaces between the words. It truly was "The Word" of YHVH. However, around the year 600 A.D., a group called the Masoretes put together and formalized a "vowel pointing" system for the Bible based on how it had been traditionally read.

Exodus 3:15 – *"…And said moreover God unto Moses, Thus shall you say unto the sons of Israel: The LORD* [in Hebrew, the name **Yahweh**], *the God of your fathers, the God of Abraham…has sent me unto you, **this is my name forever and this is my memorial from generation to generation"*** (Interlinear Bible paraphrase, emphasis mine).

Now, whenever you see the name LORD written in all caps in the Old Testament, or the Old Testament quoted in the New Testament, it is the Hebrew personal name of the Father which is **Yahweh**. However, what is written in nearly all English Bibles is the title, the LORD, which is not His name. YHVH is the **Lord (of all)**, but that is not His personal name.

The translators did the world a huge injustice and were simply in error when they removed the Father's holy name and the actual name of His Son from the English translations of the Bible. This kept the real personal name of the only true God from the readers. Without His personal name, YHVH became known by the generic moniker, "God."

There is also a Hebrew/Jewish doctrine of not using or pronouncing the name of YHVH, except on high holy days. This doctrine, called *ineffability*, proposes that God's name is too holy to be pronounced except on special occasions. However, it is difficult to understand why this tradition would come into being when Hebrew Scripture itself says:

Joel 2:32 – *"…Whoever will call on the name of Yahweh shall be saved…"* (WEB).

Jeremiah 10:6 – *"There is none like you, Yahweh; you are great, and your name is great in might"* (WEB).

Indeed, the only command regarding His name in the Torah is in the Ten Commandments and states:

Exodus 20:7 – *"You shall not take the name of Yahweh your God in vain…"* (WEB).

So, the command is to simply not misuse or to take in vain the name of *Yahweh*.

Even more troubling and confusing is that the generic name "lord" is also used for the pagan god, Baal. By using the generic name "Lord," it does not differentiate Him from any of the gods of any other religion. Think about it for a moment: Every other religion has a name for their god, i.e. Allah, Buddha, etc., but to an outsider it would seem that Christians do not know the name of their own—the one and only true God, *Yahweh*. Not every god that people recognize as god, **is** the true God of the Bible.

Translator Error

Further, it was simple translator error to not reveal His name. There is an accepted principle that virtually every other translator follows, and that is *translation* vs. *transliteration*. The accepted rule is that when you are translating a text, you attempt to convey the meaning that would be best understood by your audience. With this understanding, readers realize that they may not be getting a word-for-word transliteration of the text, but rather words that best communicates the underlying ideas in their own languages.

However, whenever proper nouns (people's names and places) are converted to the new language, they are to be transliterated. This means they are converted to the new language exactly intact! For instance, if my name, Alan, is converted to Hebrew it would be—Alan! This is a proper transliteration. If converted to Russian, Spanish, French, or German, it would still be Alan.

As further proof of what I mean, just listen to any Spanish television station that is broadcasting a Dallas Cowboys game, or any other American team. The same principle is used. You will hear everything entirely in Spanish until a player's name is spoken. For example, you might hear, "Jason Witten *puntuaciones!*" (Jason Witten scores!) The broadcaster will always use his American name. His name, as a proper noun, is transliterated.

Why the translators of the Bible did not adhere to this rule, I will let that be for you to decide. Suffice it to say, because all the Hebrew names have a meaning behind them, we lose out on much of the richness of the Bible. For instance, the English name for our Savior is Jesus, yet this name does not have a specific meaning attached to it. On the other hand, Jesus' Hebrew name is *Yehoshua*, or *Yeshua*, which can alternately mean "Yah[weh] saves," or "salvation." Another example is the prophet Micah's name. Again, this English derivation of the prophet's actual name has no meaning. However, in Hebrew the name is spelled *Mikhayu* and means "who is like *Yahweh*."

So, be aware that whenever you see "LORD," in all caps in your Bible, it is His personal name, *Yahweh*. Now, please do not get religious (a word that actually means bondage) and think that you have to use this name all the time, or that you are not saved unless you have used this name, or worse, that you are somehow more spiritual if you use this name. If you believe you are more spiritual because of something you have done it is usually an indication of a religious spirit, and Jesus is not religious. Jesus does not bring bondage, but freedom (Galatians 5:1).

Our goal, as Believers, is not to be religious, but to be like Jesus: strong, yet humble. In fact, if you look at His life, you will see that it was the religious Pharisees and Sadducees that Jesus was typically angry with. As Believers, we are all part of His Body, so let us walk in love and humility toward one another and the world, not in pride.

However, it is good to know, as a matter of biblical literacy, that the Bible states in the Old Testament that the Father's people will know His name. But it does not mean someone is not saved if they do not know it, as the New Covenant is all about Jesus and knowing Him! Jesus is the door to the Father, and no one goes to the Father except through Him (John 14:6).

Isaiah 52:6 – *"Therefore my people shall know my name: therefore [they shall know] in that day that I [am] he that doth speak: behold, [it is] I"* (KJV).

Jeremiah 16:21 – *"Therefore, behold, I will this once cause them to know, I will cause them to know mine hand and my might; and they shall know that my name [is] The LORD"* (KJV, Interlinear Bible renders "the LORD," *Yahweh*.)

Incidentally, knowing that LORD is the name *Yahweh*, has an additional benefit. With this tidbit of knowledge, you can also prove that Jesus is God. In Matthew 3:3, John the Baptist quotes Isaiah 40:3, where Isaiah prophesied (700 YEARS before Jesus' birth) about John the Baptist, and who John would be announcing: *"The voice of one crying in the wilderness, make ready the way of the LORD."*

In Hebrew, Isaiah 40:3 is rendered, "make ready the way of *Yahweh*." John the Baptist, in Matthew 3:3, announced the coming of Jesus, but quoted a Scripture where Isaiah proclaimed that the One who is coming is *Yahweh*! Therefore, **Jesus is YAHWEH—God**! Most people will read Matthew 3:3 and gloss right over this Scripture, but now that you know that LORD means *Yahweh*, you can see the truth hidden in plain sight: Jesus and *Yahweh* are one. This can be a great witnessing tool that anyone can use, especially with our Jewish friends. Halleluyah!

As a final point regarding the name of the Father, it is an amazing historical fact that because of the love that the Father had for His Son, God placed His name, the Tetragrammaton (YHVH) over the cross, front and center at the crucifixion. To make the event even more amazing, God made the pagan Roman governor, Pontius Pilate, responsible for placing His name, YHVH, over His Son. Pilate ruled over the Jews and Romans who were carrying out this heinous deed. He thought he was the ultimate authority in that place, yet, God made him His errand boy to make this hidden-in-plain-sight statement of His love and affirmation of His Son, written in Hebrew:

John 19:19-21 – *"*¹⁹*Pilate wrote a title also, and put it on the cross. There was written, "JESUS OF NAZARETH, THE KING OF THE JEWS."* ²⁰*Therefore many of the Jews read this title, for the place where Jesus was crucified was near the city; and it was written in Hebrew, in Latin, and in Greek.* ²¹*The chief priests of the Jews therefore said to Pilate, "Don't write, 'The King of the Jews,' but, 'he said, I am King of the Jews'""* (WEB).

As the Roman Governor, Pontius Pilate could have changed the inscription, but instead left it saying, "What I have written, I have written" (John 19:22).

The reason the Jews were so vehemently upset was because the inscription, in Hebrew, spelled out the acrostic below:

Yeshua **H**a'Nazari **V**emelech **H**ay'hudim

Yes, in the most ignominious moment of Jesus' life, His Heavenly Father placed His personal name, YHVH, over His Son. God was declaring in plain sight, both to everyone in attendance and—because it is recorded in the Scriptures—to everyone who lives throughout history, exactly who Jesus was. It was God's personal stamp of approval, acceptance, and affirmation on His Son, even when it seemed to the world that Yeshua had been defeated. By placing His Name over His Son, the Father was effectively repeating the same words that He had spoken to His Son two other times while He was on Earth.

Approval, Acceptance, & Affirmation

The affirming words the Father spoke in the Scriptures below are so powerful that they empowered Yeshua's entire ministry. The first time they were spoken by the Father to Jesus, was at His baptism (in the Jordan River near the Dead Sea, the lowest point in Israel, and on Earth). The second time was at His trans-figuration (on Mount Hermon, the highest point in Israel), with Peter, James and John as witnesses.

The composite picture, for all born-again Believers, is that whether you are at a low point in your life, or a high point in your life, the Father is pleased with you because He sees you in Christ.

Matthew 3:17 – *"Behold, a voice out of the heavens said, "This is my beloved Son, with whom I am well pleased""* (WEB).

Matthew 17:5 – *"While he was still speaking, behold, a bright cloud overshadowed them. Behold, a voice came out of the cloud,* *saying, "This is my beloved Son, in whom I am well pleased. Listen to him""* (WEB).

The words in the Scriptures above are also the words that the Father wants every Believer to realize are also true for them. They are now true and being said to every Believer by the Father. Because you are in Christ, hear them being said to you now, "I, your name, am the Father's beloved son/daughter, in whom He is well pleased!" If these words empowered Yeshua's ministry and life, they are also designed to empower yours when they become real for you! After all, you are part of the Body of Christ!

Supremacy of Grace at the Transfiguration

Referencing Matthew 17, there are also a couple of pictures of the supremacy of grace (the New Covenant) over the Mosaic Law that are hidden in plain sight in the narrative of the transfiguration story. The first picture is more obvious, as the Scripture states that Moses (who represents the Mosaic Law), and Elijah (who represents the Prophets), appeared to them, talking with Jesus. In verse five, the Father speaks and states, *"This is my beloved Son, in whom I am well pleased; hear ye Him!"*

Amazingly, God does not even bother to recognize Moses or Elijah but focuses His attention exclusively on His Son and tells the three disciples in attendance to hear Him! What a message this is for our own lives. The verbal picture here is that **Jesus is superior to, and takes preeminence over, the Mosaic Law and the Prophets.** We are to hear Him above all others.

In other words, Jesus, and His New Covenant, trumps the Old Testament Mosaic Law and Prophets. No, I am not saying we should ignore the Mosaic Law and the Prophets. However, what we should do is ask the Father to show us the pictures of Jesus there, as the Old Covenant is the New Covenant concealed, just as the New Covenant is the Old Covenant revealed. In addition, an important point to remember is that Scripture states that Jesus is mediator (meaning; peacemaker or intercessor) only of the New Covenant. His blood was spilled only for the New

Covenant, which is a better covenant than the Old (Hebrews 9:15, Hebrews 12:24 Hebrews 8:6). So, if you are trying to obey the Ten Commandments or any of the Mosaic Law, you are doing it alone, as Jesus is not the mediator of the Mosaic Covenant.

The, second picture is hidden in the names of the disciples who accompanied Jesus: Peter James and John. It is specifically because the Father said, "...hear Him," (Jesus) and not the Mosaic Law/Torah (Moses), or the Prophets (Elijah), that the disciple's names become important. Let us look at the precision of Scripture and break down the names in the order that they appear.

Matthew 17:1 – *"And after six days Jesus taketh Peter, James, and John his brother, and bringeth them up into a high mountain apart"* (KJV).

Peter's name, in Hebrew, is *Kepha,* and means "stone"; James's name, in Hebrew, is *Yackov,* and means "supplanter"; John's name, in Hebrew, is *Yochannan* and means "grace." The hidden message in this story is prophetic of Jesus and the preeminence of His covenant. Peter's name, *Kepha,* or stone, is representative of the 10 Commandments, the Mosaic Law, as they were written on stones. So, the message and picture is:

The Mosaic Law has been Supplanted by Grace!

The Bible is literally littered with these types of pictures showing the preeminence of Jesus and His Grace Covenant over the Mosaic Law Covenant, and we will discover them if we ask the Holy Spirit to reveal them to us.

However, the final—and to me the most amazing— picture is hidden in the word *Torah,* itself. The very Hebrew word that was translated "Law," is also a prophetic utterance of the New Covenant to come and a picture of the preeminence of Jesus in its establishment. Here is what I mean, as we break down the word *Torah.*

As stated earlier, there are no vowels in the original Hebrew language, and every Hebrew letter has both a corresponding numerical value and pictogram, or picture. If we look at the consonants in the word, *Torah*, we will find a hidden gem of a message. The letter T, or *Tav*, is the last letter of the Hebrew aleph-bet and has the picture of the cross. The letter R, or *Resh*, and means the head or the beginning. The letter H or *Hey*, is a picture of someone looking out a window, and means grace.

Therefore, the ironic message found hidden in the word *Torah*—the very word that was translated Law—is that it actually means "The cross is the beginning of grace!" More to the point, grace had its beginning at the cross! So, we see that hidden in the very word that denotes the Old Covenant Mosaic Law, *Torah*, God points us to Jesus and grace.

THE CROSS (JESUS) IS THE BEGINNING OF GRACE!

Alpha and Omega

You may also recall that Jesus said in the book of Revelation that He is the *Alpha* and the *Omega*, or the First and the Last, or the Beginning and the End. This description loses much of its meaning in the Greek. In Hebrew, Jesus is not only saying He is the *Aleph* and the *Tav*, or the Beginning and End. Since these two letters are also the first and last letters of the Hebrew aleph-bet, He is saying that He is the First and the Last—He is the all in all!

In addition, when we overlay these two letters with the Old and New Covenant, we discover something else quite interesting. The first letter of the Hebrew aleph-bet is *Aleph*, and its picture is that of an ox, and symbolizes work. The last letter, as mentioned above, is *Tav*, and its picture is the cross. Amazingly, the first covenant, was indeed the covenant of the ox, works! The last covenant is a covenant of grace, and is symbolized by the cross, which is the end of work(s)!

Abba (Hebrew for Daddy) is wonderful, is He not?

Works vs. Grace

Now let's examine the Old Covenant. If the Hebrews, the people of YHVH in the Old Covenant, would perform the terms of the covenant **then** God would fulfill His part. If they sinned, the sacrificial system would bring them back into "right standing" with God.

So, the essence of the Old Covenant was based on man's performance as they knew that the Father, being infallible, would perform His part. This is the foundation of the Old Covenant. It centered on man's performance: i.e. Man Does Good = Man Gets Good; Man Does Bad = Man Gets Bad. However, man—in the form of the nation of Israel—tried for nearly 1500 years and was not able to attain the Father's righteousness through their works.

The blood of bulls and goats, being offered morning and afternoon, once per year on Yom Kippur, Feast of Atonement, and multiple other times, was a temporary and ineffective solution.

Hebrews 10:4 – *"For it is impossible for the blood of bulls and goats should take away sins"* (WEB).

So, God, in His mercy, offered a permanent solution. His Son offered Himself as a perfect sacrifice for sin: *Yahweh* and man in One Person, Yeshua/Jesus. He was a man with a double claim to the throne of King David of Israel, because He could trace His lineage back from His mother, Mary, to King David's son Nathan, and also from His earthly father Joseph (though the Seed was provided by the Holy Spirit) to David's son Solomon. Therefore, He met the Jews' qualifications of their promised Jewish *Mashiach* (Messiah). He was, as John the Baptist proclaimed:

John 1:29 – *"…The Lamb of God, who takes away the sin of the world!"* (WEB).

His one-time sacrifice would fulfill—do away with the necessity of—all of the sacrifices that the Jews were required to make. Essentially, Jesus' sacrifice was one sacrifice to rule them all, as His sacrifice was once and for all!

Hebrews 9:26 – *"…But now once at the end of the ages, he has been revealed to put away sin by the sacrifice of himself"* (WEB).

So, the New Covenant is based exclusively on what Jesus did for us through His cross, His resurrection and the giving of His Holy Spirit. It is not based on anything man does, except to believe on His finished work.

Ephesians 2:8-9 – *"8For by grace you have been saved through faith, and that not of yourselves; it is the gift of God, 9not of works, that no one would boast"* (WEB).

Our part is to simply believe in Him and all that He has done. The almost too-good-to-be-true news is this: Once you have the humility and common sense to admit you are a sinner, accepted the blood of Jesus as the sacrifice for your sins, and given your heart to Him, you will have become a born-again Believer and part of the Father's family, forever.

Hebrews 9:22 – *"…and without shedding of blood there is no remission"* (NKJV).

John 3:3, 5-7 – *"3Jesus answered…Verily, verily, I say unto thee, Except a man be born again, he cannot see the kingdom of God… 5Jesus answered, Verily, verily, I say unto thee, Except a man be born of water and of the Spirit, he cannot enter into the kingdom of God. 6That which is born of the flesh is flesh; and that which is born of the Spirit is spirit. 7Marvel not that I said unto thee, Ye must be born again"* (KJV).

You, without any works or righteous deeds of your own, have been made righteous for free by His blood, and the devil has no power to snatch you out of God's hand.

John 10:28-29 – *"28I give eternal life to them. They will never perish, and no one will snatch them out of my hand. 29My Father,* *who has given them to me, is greater than all. No one is able to snatch them out of my Father's hand"* (WEB).

Why Salvation

Before continuing, and in the interest of laying a complete foundation, we should explain why there was even a need for salvation, and a New Covenant, to begin with. The reason why every man and woman in the world needs Jesus is because of sin. This is the "red letter" topic that most the world does not want to talk about today. They would rather just say, "I have an issue with (X) problem." What is seldom talked about today in our politically correct environment is that every person born into this world, even though they have not done anything good or bad, is born a sinner. This is a result of the sin of our original father, Adam.

Romans 5:12 – *"Wherefore, as by one man sin entered into the world, and death by sin; and so death passed upon all men, for that all have sinned"* (KJV).

However, Hebrews 10:12 declares that Jesus *"...offered one sacrifice for sins forever..."* So, once you accept Jesus as your once and forever sin offering, you have been reconciled to your Father in Heaven and have been made righteous and justified by Jesus forever!

Romans 5:17-19 – *"[17]For if by one man's offence death reigned by one; much more they which receive abundance of grace and of the gift of righteousness shall reign in life by one, Jesus Christ.) [18]Therefore as by the offence of one judgment came upon all men to condemnation; even so by the righteousness of one the free gift came upon all men unto justification of life. [19]For as by one man's disobedience many were made sinners, so by the obedience of one shall many be made righteous"* (KJV).

So, from the two previous Scriptures from Romans, let us understand this following reality: We are not sinners because we sin; we sin because we are sinners. We are all born sons of Adam, and that is why we are all sinners.

I understand that it may be frustrating and even offensive to many people to believe that we were all born sinners just by being descendants of Adam, but the reality is that we inherited the condition of our original father. Most people believe that they are good. At worst, they believe, "I may not be perfect, but I have not murdered anyone or committed (name your sin here), and I am sure not as bad as so-and-so."

In our logical minds, it just does not make sense. You may be asking yourself, "How can I be guilty of something if I have not done anything?" When we think about guilt we naturally tend to think of our laws, our courts, and our judicial system. In nearly every culture on Earth, you have to have done something in order to be guilty. However, to understand the spiritual reality of being born a sinner it is helpful to move from a judicial mindset to a medical mindset.

To illustrate what I mean, let's take the natural example of a baby who inherits a genetic defect from his parents. The baby has not done anything deserving of the genetic defect, however, immediately at birth, or over the course of time, the defect will manifest. Hopefully, now you can easily see the correlation to our spiritual condition.

Spiritually speaking, our sin nature was simply inherited from our father, Adam. This Biblical truth flies in the face of many false religions, or false teachings, about the truth of our spiritual condition at birth. This is a deception of the devil, because if he can get the world to believe there is no such thing as sin, he can keep the world from seeking Jesus as a remedy for sin. What is interesting about these false teachings is that, if you research them, you will find that nearly all of them have (either at their core or as one of their tenants) one, or all of the following heretical themes:

1) "There is no such thing as sin, therefore I could not be sinful at birth."

2) "We are perfect at birth and it is life (i.e. my upbringing or what has happened to me) that has

made me as I am. Therefore, I must now research and get more knowledge to "fix" myself,[1] and eventually **I will** achieve (or as some false religions term it, ascend) and be at peace, have money, power, fame etc." Well, we find the identity of who originally uttered this phrase by referencing the following passage of Scripture:

Isaiah 14:12-15 – *"12How art thou fallen from heaven, O Lucifer, son of the morning! How art thou cut down to the ground, which didst weakened the nations! 13For thou hast said in thine heart, **I will ascend** into heaven, **I will** exalt my throne above the stars of God; **I will** also sit upon the mount of the congregation, in the sides of the north: 14**I will ascend** above the heights of the clouds; **I will be like the most High.** 15Yet thou shall be brought down to hell, to the sides of the pit"* (KJV, emphasis mine).

Do you see a pattern here? Not only is the focus on self, but Lucifer is saying, "I will be omniscient, omnipresent, and omnipotent." Many people in false belief systems or religions are saying the same thing.

3) "There is no personal God, therefore there is no absolute truth, so people should do what seems good for themselves." Those who cling to this philosophy believe that everyone should do what makes themselves happy. They are saying, in essence, they are a God unto themselves. However, in John 14:6 Jesus said, "I am the way, the truth, and the life, no one comes to the Father except through me." Acts 4:12 also states, "Nor is there salvation in any other, for there is no other name under heaven given among men by which we must be saved."

---

[1] It was the Tree of **Knowledge** of good and evil that started this entire mess! Seeking worldly knowledge is never the answer (Genesis 2-3).

4) "Through my own positive thoughts, I create my own reality; therefore, I am God." They may not state it explicitly, but this is the end-game and conclusion of this mindset.

5) "The universe (may the Force be with you) is God, not a personal God who loves me. I just need to learn about it and then manipulate it for my purposes or get in harmony with it so I can figure it out." In other words, they believe, "If I send out love, I get love." But this love does not originate from a loving, Heavenly Father, but from themselves.

All of these false beliefs have one person as their flawed central character—SELF.

There is an additional, and I believe humorous, side-note regarding the teaching or belief system that says that we are born perfect, or sinless. I suggest anyone subscribing to this belief system should be around a two-year-old child when they have been caught doing something they should not have been doing. The two-year-old will look at you with his angelic face, look you straight in the eye—smile—and then will **lie effortlessly** to try and cover up their misdeed. This is hardly a picture of sinless perfection.

Now, back to the issue of our salvation. Salvation has come, and God, for His part through Jesus, has forgiven the entire world:

1 John 2:2 – *"And he is the propitiation for our sins: and not for ours only, but also for the sins of the whole world"* (KJV).

However, please understand this important point: it is still up to man to accept God's forgiveness. We are responsible, as free moral agents on this earth, to accept the offer of salvation that has been extended to us. What keeps many people away from God is the realization that they have fallen short of God's righteousness. Scripture actually agrees with them, as it is written:

Romans 3:23 – *"for all have sinned, and fall short of the glory of God"* (WEB).

Deep down they know they cannot achieve the Father's standard of righteousness, and they know that they are in sin, so they think the Father is angry with them. Friend, I have good news for you: The Scripture states that it is not your righteous deeds that get you to Heaven. It is the one righteous deed, and righteousness, of Jesus, the Messiah. Here is further proof:

Romans 3:21-24 – *"21But now the righteousness of God **without the law** is manifested, being witnessed by the law and the prophets; 22Even the righteousness of God which is by faith of Jesus Christ unto all and upon all them that believe: for there is no difference: 23For all have sinned, and come short of the glory of God; 24Being justified freely by his grace through the redemption that is in Christ Jesus"* (KJV, emphasis mine).

What every reader of this book needs to understand is that, because of the blood sacrifice of Jesus, no matter what you have done, your sin debt has been paid in full forever, and your Father in Heaven is not mad at you. He loves you and wants His absolute best for you, and the Father's best is found in union with His Son, Jesus.

1 Corinthians 6:17 – *"But he who is joined to the Lord is one spirit"* (WEB).

The life He desires you to have is to be directed by His Holy Spirit, with whom Jesus himself baptizes you.

John 1:33 – *"...Upon whom thou shalt see the Spirit descending, and remaining on him, the same is he which baptizeth with the Holy Ghost"* (KJV).

In general, we see that there are two groups of people who refuse to humble themselves before the Messiah, Jesus. These two are aside from the atheist who does not even believe in God, and of whom God said this:

Psalm 14:1 – *"The fool has said in his heart, "There is no God""* (WEB).

Psalm 53:1 – *"The fool has said in his heart, "There is no God""* (WEB).

Proverbs 9:10 – *"The fear of Yahweh is the beginning of wisdom…"*(WEB).

So, aside from the atheist, there is first the person who believes they can find their own way to the Father, that they are fine without Him (pride; self-righteousness), or that they have done enough good works, thereby deserving Heaven based upon their own merit. On the other end of the spectrum, there is the second type of person who believes that they are too sinful to be forgiven, so they feel unworthy of coming to Him.

Many people would say that the latter person is humble—so humble that they do not believe they can come to God. However, this person is also deceived by pride, just like the first, yet here it is a false pride. Why? In essence, this person has a higher opinion of their sins than the blood of Yeshua, which is over and higher than all things! They are actually extoling their sins and puffing them up, which is the definition of the word pride. Both of these people are in pride and error, but the Scriptures below contain the truth:

Romans 6:23 – *"For the wages of sin is death, but the free gift of God is eternal life in Christ Jesus our Lord"* (WEB).

Romans 10:10 – *"For with the heart one **believes** unto righteousness; and with the mouth confession is made unto salvation"* (WEB, emphasis mine).

Ephesians 2:8-9 – *"⁸for by grace you have been saved through faith, and that not of yourselves; it is the gift of God, ⁹not of works that no one would boast"* (WEB).

If you have not done so, humble yourself to Yeshua now and give Him your heart (and thereby your life), and accept His free offer of salvation!

John 14:23 – *"…My Father will love him, and we will come to him, and make our home with him"* (WEB).

Repentance: Metanoia vs. T'shuvah

Since we are discussing salvation, let me also offer some additional information about a relevant component to this: Repentance. Most Bible scholars, when teaching or writing on this subject (since the New Testament was written in Greek) will focus on the Greek word for repentance, *metanoia*. However, we need to examine both the Greek and Hebrew word for repentance, *t'shuvah*, to gain proper understanding of what these words mean.

First, let's consider the Greek *metanoia*. This word carries with it the implication of making a new decision, to turn around, or to face a new direction. Some have simplified it by saying it is simply to change your mind.

While this definition is not at all error, it can put the person in a box, or on a hamster wheel that they cannot escape. It places the emphasis back on the person's action of changing the mind, rather than on Yeshua, where it belongs. Remember, this covenant is not about us; it is all about Him and our position in Him.

What do I mean by this? If I am dealing with an issue in my life that I cannot seem to get victory over, I will constantly be telling myself, "**I** just need to repent, (change my mind, make a new decision) about this and it will be better. I need to do it!" Over and over it goes, we sin and repent, sin and repent. When we do not see change, we are back on that hamster wheel of performance.

This puts the emphasis on me, and my mind, and my abilities. This mentality can devolve into a works (i.e. Law/Legalism) mentality where it is up to me to do all of the work of overcoming an area of weakness in my life.

Now, please understand, obviously your will **is** involved and needs to be exercised. But remember, how did you get saved? It was by His grace. We need to see that the way we got saved, which was by grace, is also the way to holiness and godliness in our lives.

Romans 6:14 – *"For sin will not have dominion over you. For you are not under law, but under grace"* (WEB).

If we slip back into our performance, we have fallen from grace and are back under the Mosaic Law and legalism, which we will see below is the **ministry of death**! Yes, the Apostle Paul calls the Ten Commandments the ministry of death.

2 Corinthians 3:7-8 – *"7But if the ministry of death, written and engraved on stones, was glorious...which glory was passing away, 8how will the ministry of the Spirit not be more glorious?"* (NKJV).

THE ONLY PART OF THE MOSAIC LAW THAT WAS ENGRAVED ON STONES WAS THE TEN COMMANDMENTS.

Going back to the definition of metanoia, it tells us **to turn from**, but what are we to **turn to**? The weakness of this word and its definition is that the new direction that the word *metanoia* turns us toward is back to ourselves and our efforts, and that is not going to work because it was **us** (our flesh) that was the problem in the first place!

So, is there a word that can give us a deeper understanding of what New Covenant repentance is supposed to look like? In my study of the Hebrew language, I think there is, and I think it will be a real eye opener for you and bless your socks off.

The word for repentance in Hebrew is *t'shuvah*. If we break down the meaning of this word, it divides into two parts. The first part is simply the Hebrew word *shuv,* which means "return." For example, if you were in Israel today, and you saw a mother motioning for her children to come inside, or to return, the word she would yell is, "*Shuv!* Children, *shuv!*"

The second part of this word is the most interesting part, as the AH, or H, is used at the end of many words in Hebrew, especially with people's names. For example: Isaiah, Amaziah, Hezekiah, Micah, Zechariah and Jeremiah. As I mentioned previously, the Hebrew language is unique in the world. It has twenty-two letters and no vowels. Each letter also represents both a number and a corresponding pictogram, or a picture. The pictogram that goes with the letter H is the picture of a man looking out of a window to the outside. The meaning of this pictogram is GRACE!

So now let us put the definition of the Hebrew word for repentance together:

SHUV = RETURN; and *AH, H,* = GRACE!

The meaning of repentance, in Hebrew is RETURN TO GRACE!

The question is: Who has extended grace and forgiven the world and who is the personification of grace? It is none other than our Savior, The Lamb of God, The Messiah, The Prince of Peace, Yeshua, Jesus!

John 1:17 – *"For the law was given through Moses, but **grace** and **truth** came through Jesus Christ"* (NKJV, emphasis mine).

So, New Covenant repentance, after the initial repentance of salvation, is simply returning to the author and finisher of our faith, Jesus (Hebrews 12:2). It is seeing that we are forgiven, and realizing that, whenever we commit sin it is committed in the flesh (it does not defile our spirits), so we are not "sinners," as our spirits have been made perfect. 1 John 4:17 says, "*...because as he is, even so are we in this world.*"

We only need to [re]turn to Him, as it is His righteousness that cleanses us. If this is difficult to understand, there is other verbiage that might help you see how this is possible. Let us look at Jesus in Scripture, as it says that He became sin (on the cross) for us, even though He committed no sin Himself (2 Corinthians 5:21). This sounds a bit confusing doesn't it? But He became our sin offering, and all the sins of the world were placed upon Him.

On the other hand, once we are born again, we do not have a sin nature, even though we commit sins (in the flesh). Our spirits have been regenerated, which means they were made alive and brought back into unity with God.

There are some who believe that after our born again experience we never have to confess our sins again, because we are perfect in our spirits. While it is true that you are perfect in your spirit, let's listen to the words of Jesus when He went to wash Peter's feet, because this is where we get the full picture.

When Jesus came to Peter, Peter refused to let Jesus wash his feet. Jesus told Peter that if he did not allow Him to do so, he had no part with Him. Peter then went to the other extreme and told Jesus to wash not only his feet, but also his hands and head. Jesus then told Peter:

John 13:10 – *"...**Someone who has bathed** only needs to have **his feet washed**, but is completely clean. You are clean, but not all of you"* (WEB, emphasis mine).

Jesus is saying here that once you are saved, you are washed. If you sin subsequent to salvation, you do not need to get saved all over again. Simply acknowledge your sins (wash your feet) to the Father and thank Him for the forgiveness that is already yours! When Jesus said, *"Ye are clean, but not all,"* He was referring to Judas Iscariot, who would betray Him.

Spirt, Soul and Body: What Happens When I Am Born Again?

It will be worthwhile, at this point, to explain what happens when you are born again. We must understand that man is a three part being: He is spirit, soul, and body.

2 Thessalonians 5:23 – *"May the god of peace himself sanctify you completely. May your whole* **spirit, soul, and body** *be preserved blameless at the coming of our Lord Jesus Christ"* (WEB, emphasis mine).

It has been said this way: Man is a spirit, he possesses a soul, and lives in a body. When you are born again by the Spirit of God it is your spirit that gets born again and it is made just as perfect as Jesus is. Does that surprise you? There is Scripture to prove it!

1 John 4:17 – *"…because* **as he is, even so are we IN THIS WORLD***"* (WEB, emphasis mine).

Notice, it does not say when we die and go to be with Him, but now, in this world, we are as He is in our spirits.

2 Corinthians 5:17 – *"Therefore if anyone is in Christ, he is a new creation. The old things have passed away. Behold, all things have become new"* (WEB).

You see, our souls (our minds, wills and emotions) are not immediately made perfect.

Romans 12:2 – *"Don't be conformed to this world,* **but be transformed by the renewing of your mind,** *so that you may prove what is the good, well-pleasing, and perfect will of God"* (WEB, emphasis mine).

Once we are born again, we are to renew our minds with the Word of God by reading and meditating on it. Finally, regarding our bodies, if you look in the mirror after you are born again, you will probably realize that our bodies were also not made perfect by accepting Jesus as Savior. However, that too is coming when He returns.

1 Corinthians 15:54 – *"...when this corruptible has put on incorruption..."* (NKJV).

It is the spirit part of you that was born again and that was made perfect! This is the confusing part for many Believers. They think, *Well, I am born again, so why am I still having bad thoughts? Why do I still have evil desires?* Friend, relax. As you yield to God, you are being changed from the inside out and usually most of our behavior does not change overnight. You will not change by the force of your will—that is what the Old Covenant and its mindset was all about. Change under the Old Covenant was possible, but it was always short-lived, because it was human effort doing it. At that time, the spirits of men could not yet be in union with God's Spirit as they can now in the New Covenant.

1 Corinthians 6:17 – *"But whoever is united with the Lord is one with him in spirit"* (NIV).

This is important point to grasp. You are one spirit with God when you are born again by His Spirit. When you are born again by His Spirit, God now lives inside you!

The ironic thing is that this free gift is passed up every day. In most cases, the reason is because people do not know that it is indeed free. It is not based on your obedience or your goodness! Let me restate that again. You, on your own, can never be good enough, pure enough, give enough money to charity, or do enough good works to merit going to Heaven.

Isaiah 64:6 – *"...all our righteousnesses are as filthy rags..."* (KJV).

Wonderfully though, the old saying is true: "It is not, what you know, it is who you know." Many people wrongly believe that you have to be good before you can be saved. However, they could not be more wrong. You could be the worst, most prolific sinner (all sin is wrong, but some sins have heavier consequences than others) in the world (a murderer, gangster, prostitute, or drug addict), but you can be saved without having obeyed a single one of the Ten Commandments. This boggles the natural mind because we are programmed from birth that we must "earn" things. But the truth is, we only have to be repentant. The Father simply says, "Come to me through My Son."

Jesus Himself said:

John 14:6 – *"...I am the way, the truth, and the life. No one comes to the Father except through me"* (WEB).

Matt 11:28 – *"Come to Me, all you who labor and are heavy laden, and I will give you rest"* (NKJV).

Most of the world, incorrectly, believes that you need to "get yourself right" before you come to the Father. This is a lie propagated by the devil to keep people away from our Father (our Daddy), who loves us with a perfect love. We are to come to the Father first, be born again through His Son, Jesus, and then let the grace of God change us from the inside out.

This is the very opposite of what the Old Covenant was about. It was all about first doing righteous behavior. Again, the Old Covenant was only concerned about the outside. However, the Mosaic Law could not change your heart by renewing your spirit and linking it back up in union with God.

One of the confusing things about getting rid of the Mosaic Law in its entirety, is that many Bible teachers and pastors world-wide teach that the Mosaic Law has been done away with, except for what they call "the moral" Mosaic Law, the Ten Commandments.

First of all, according to Scripture, the Torah, or Mosaic Law, was given by God as one body of work. It was not given to

Moses in bits. Many pastors and Bible teachers errantly attempt to divide the Mosaic Law into different categories. They will speak of the Ceremonial Law, as though it is separate from the Moral Law or the Civil Law. However, YHVH God never made this distinction. Trying to divide the Mosaic Law into separate categories is a construct of man. They did this as an attempt to better understand the Mosaic Law by segregating it into divisions of what they believe were the greater moral laws, which they contend are still in force, and the lesser dietary and civil laws, which they contend are no longer to be followed. This man-made division was not done within the context of what God gave to Moses. The Torah, which included the Ten Commandments, was one body of work that God gave to Moses to show Israel how God wanted them to live.

The point is that you cannot say out of one side of your mouth that the Mosaic Law has been fulfilled, and then out of the other side of your mouth say that the Ten Commandments are still in force. The simple reason that the Ten Commandments have been done away with for Believers in Jesus is because they are part of the Torah, the Mosaic Law that Jesus fulfilled. We are now, as sons, to obey from a heart of love for the Father.

If you think about this in the same way as you would a natural family, it is easily understood. You do not want your children to obey a list of rules you have made (the Old Covenant). You want them to obey you because they love you (the New Covenant). The Scripture below defines what Paul called the Ten Commandments:

2 Corinthians 3:7 – *"...the ministry of death, written and engraved on stones..."* (NKJV).

The Ten Commandments were the ONLY part of the Torah written on stones.

If these words are too overwhelming, and seem almost too good to be true, then let me share with you two pictures so that you can see two simple truths. The first picture will be of the Feast of Passover and the Feast of Shavuot, or Pentecost, in the Old Covenant. The second picture will be of these same feasts in the New Covenant. These pictures will simplify, but also make a powerful visual statement, of what the Father has done for us through Jesus.

Chapter Two
The Old Covenant Passover and Pentecost

O kay, here is where things really start to get exciting. To fully understand the freedom that a New Covenant, born-again Believer possesses, let's take a look at where we have come from. Let's consider the Old Covenant and the bondage that is inherent with it.

The Old Covenant Picture

First consider the Feast of Passover. Most people have read the story of the first Passover (in Hebrew, Pesach), or at the very least they have seen the 1956 version of *The Ten Commandments*, starring Charlton Heston. The story unfolds as the children of Israel were to take a perfect lamb on the tenth of the month and observe it for four days, to make sure it had no blemishes. Then, on the fourteenth day, they were to kill it and place some of the blood on the doorposts and lintels (top of the doorway) of their homes. By doing this they would avoid the plague of death that was coming upon Egypt.

Note that the markings of blood on the top of the doorway and its sides actually form *chet*, the eighth letter of the Hebrew alphabet:

The pictogram, or picture, that goes with this Hebrew letter is fence or separation. God, through the blood of the perfect lamb(s), was literally about to fence off, or separate, His people, Israel, from the world and world system, their Egyptian taskmasters, to whom they were enslaved.

On that first Passover night, God's people, who had applied the blood, were separated from the Egyptians when the death angel passed over them. Those who had the blood on their dwelling found life, while those who did not have the blood were visited by death.

Let's look closer and see the New Covenant picture here in the Old Covenant. In the same way, when anyone appropriates the blood of the New Covenant Lamb, Jesus, to their lives, they are also separated from the world to which they were once enslaved. Now, through this new covenant, they have everlasting life.

Also, by virtue of *chet* being the eighth letter (the Hebrew number eight means new beginnings), it also is representative of new beginnings, or a new start for the nation of Israel. Indeed,

Israel had their new beginning the next day when they came out of slavery.

Exodus 12:2-3, 5-7, 13 – *"²This month shall be to you the beginning of months. It shall be the first month of the year to you.*

³Speak to all the congregation of Israel, saying, 'On the tenth day of this month, they shall take to them every man a lamb, according to their fathers' houses, a lamb for a household…

⁵Your lamb shall be without defect [blemish], *a male a year old…*

⁶and you shall keep it until the fourteenth day of the same month; and the whole assembly of the congregation of Israel shall kill it at evening.

⁷They shall take some of the blood, and put it on the two door posts and on the lintel, on the houses in which they shall eat it…

¹³The blood shall be to you for a token on the houses where you are: and when I see the blood, I will pass over you, and there shall no plague be on you to destroy you, when I strike the land of Egypt" (WEB).

A blood covenant was the most serious type of agreement that could be entered into in middle-eastern culture. The blood of the blood covenant was always a sign of the seriousness of the agreement because, *"life is in the blood"* (Leviticus 17:11). The blood of the lamb on the outside of the homes signified the beginning of the covenant, as YHVH was taking the nation of Israel unto Himself. The terms of this blood covenant would be agreed to by Israel which would make them legally liable to perform all that was in the covenant. When they fell short in the performance of the covenant, they would bear the consequences that were also detailed within that agreement.

The blood of the natural perfect lamb on their dwellings prefigures the blood of Jesus, whom John the Baptist called, *"…The Lamb of God who takes away the sin of the world!"*

John 1:29 – *"The next day John saw Jesus coming toward him, and said, "Behold! The Lamb of God who takes away the sin of the world!""* (WEB).

Just as there was protection for the Hebrews from natural death from the plague, because they applied the blood of the natural lamb to the outside of their dwellings, there is protection for all New Covenant Believers from spiritual death. We have applied the blood of Jesus, the Lamb of God, to our hearts, the inside of our dwellings, by accepting the blood of His sacrificial death for our sins.

Jesus said in John 11:25-26, *"25I am the resurrection and the life, He who believes in Me, though he may die, he shall live. 26And whoever lives and believes in Me shall never die…"*

In fact, so that there could be no doubt as to the clarity of this picture, in the book of 1 Corinthians, the Apostle Paul specifically called Jesus our Passover.

1 Corinthians 5:7 – *"…For indeed Christ, our Passover, was sacrificed for us"* (NKJV).

Another very telling Scripture about the ineffectiveness of the Old Covenant is Hebrews 10:1, where the Mosaic Law is called, *"…a shadow of the good things to come."* The question is, "How many dimensions does a shadow have?" The answer is, "Two." This again points out another weakness of the Mosaic Law. Since it was a shadow of the reality, of what Jesus would do, it could only affect a person on two of their three (spirit, soul and body) levels. The Mosaic Law could affect their souls, (the mind, will and emotions), and their bodies, but it was powerless to affect their spirits, and therein lies the problem. It could not regenerate the core of who they were, their spirits, and put them back in union with God. In essence, the Mosaic Law demanded perfection, but left them powerless to attain the very perfection it demanded!

Health and Provision in the Old Covenant

Before Passover ever happened, it is important to note that the children of Israel had been instructed by YHVH, through Moses, to ask Egypt for its gold, silver and clothing. God even had the Egyptians provide Israel's clothing for their trip (Exodus 12:35). Because of His supernatural favor on Israel, the Egyptians complied with those requests. Israel also left Egypt with not one person being feeble, as noted in Psalms 105:37.

In short, the amazing picture of what happened is that, after Passover, Israel plundered Egypt (the world system) of its gold, silver, and clothing, and left **totally healthy and healed after they had partaken of the lamb**! When you see the composite picture of what this means for the New Covenant Believer, you should be very excited: When **we** partake of the New Covenant Lamb of God, Jesus, we are given faith to believe for health and provision. After all, we have a new and better covenant, so this is not something exclusively spiritual (Hebrews 8:6). It is everything that Israel had in the natural, plus more.

Exodus 3:21-22 – *"21I will give this people favor in the sight of the Egyptians, and it will happen that when you go, you shall not go empty-handed. 22But every woman shall ask of her neighbor, and of her who visits her house, jewels of silver, jewels of gold, and clothing; and you shall put them on your sons, and on your daughters. You shall plunder the Egyptians"* (WEB).

Exodus 12: 35-36 – *"35The children of Israel did according to the word of Moses; and they asked of the Egyptians jewels of silver, and jewels of gold, and clothing. 36Yahweh gave the people favor in the sight of the Egyptians, so that they let them have what they asked. They plundered the Egyptians"* (WEB).

Psalm 105:37 – *"He brought them out with silver and gold. There was not one feeble person among his tribes"* (WEB).

The New Covenant promises revealed by these Old Covenant pictures are that you, as a Believer in God's perfect Lamb, Jesus, have an absolute right under your new and better covenant to claim financial success and divine health. It IS part of the covenant of Jesus!

Now, there is no condemnation in this next statement, but if we are not living in these blessings that were given to Old Covenant Believers, maybe we as New Covenant Believers should go back and partake of (spend time with) the Lamb.

Crossing the Red Sea to Mount Sinai

After Passover, the people of Israel left Egypt, and then came to their next significant event: The Red Sea crossing.

Exodus 14:21-23 – *"21Moses stretched out his hand over the sea, and Yahweh caused the sea to go back by a strong east wind all night, and made the sea dry land, and the waters were divided. 22The children of Israel went into the **middle of the sea** on the dry ground, and the waters were a wall to them on their right hand, and on their left. 23The Egyptians pursued, and went in after them into the middle of the sea: all of Pharaoh's horses, his chariots, and his horsemen"* (WEB, emphasis mine).

This scene of the Hebrew people going through the Red Sea, with the water as a wall on their right and left, is a picture of water baptism for the nation of Israel, after they had applied the blood of the Lamb to their dwellings. Please see that New Covenant Believers mirror this, as they are instructed to go through water baptism after they apply the blood of the Lamb of God to their hearts.

Mark 16:16 – *"He who believes and is baptized will be saved…"* (WEB).

The scene continues with Pharaoh and his Egyptian army pursuing their former slaves, YHVH's people. This is an Old Covenant representation of a New Covenant reality. The devil portrayed here in type by Pharaoh, and the world system are constantly pursuing/tempting Believers in Christ, trying to tempt us to sin (act worldly), or worse, reject the Covenant of Jesus altogether and go back to the world system, Egypt.

As a Believer, you may well feel the pull of the adversary and his world system—his kingdom—or people from your previous life, beckoning you to come back. Sometimes it is even like he is chasing you. However, the promise of God's Word is in the following Scriptures:

James 4:7 – *"Submit yourselves therefore to God. Resist the devil, and he will flee from you"* (KJV).

Ephesians 6:10 – *"Finally, my brethren, be strong in the Lord and in the power of His might"* (NKJV).

1 Corinthians 16:13 – *"Watch! Stand firm in the faith! Be courageous! Be strong!"* (WEB).

Romans 6:14 – *"For sin will not have dominion over you. For you are not under law, but under grace"* (WEB).

Just as the nation of Israel came out of Egypt, Believers in Christ have come out of the world system, and now we are **in** this world, but not **of** this world, as Jesus stated in the Gospel of John.

John 17:16 – *"They are not of the world, even as I am not of the world"* (WEB).

Once you accept Jesus as your Savior, your citizenship changes, and you are no longer primarily a citizen of this world. You are now a citizen of Heaven and ambassador for Christ, and His kingdom, to the world.

2 Corinthians 5:20-21 – *"20We are therefore ambassadors on behalf of Christ, as though God were entreating by us: we beg you on behalf of Christ, be reconciled to God. 21For him who knew no sin he made to be sin on our behalf; so that in him we might become the righteousness of God"* (WEB).

41

The Old Covenant Fifty Days

Now, the next step that we need to take, because it will become important later, is to count the number of days from the time Israel left Egypt until the time that they reached Mt. Sinai. To begin with, we know that they left Egypt on the evening of the 14th day of the first month.

Exodus 12:2 – *"This month shall be to you the beginning of months. It shall be the first month of the year to you"* (WEB).

Exodus 12:6 – *"and you shall keep it* [the lamb] *until the fourteenth day of the same month; and the whole assembly of the congregation of Israel shall kill it at evening"* (WEB, brackets mine).

To get the other needed information, we need to go to Exodus 19:1-2, and Exodus 19:11, from the New International Version of the Bible (NIV).

Exodus 19:1-2 – *"¹On the first day of the third month after the Israelites left Egypt — on that very day — they came to the Desert of Sinai. ²After they set out from Rephidim, they entered the Desert of Sinai, and Israel camped there in the desert in front of the mountain"* (NIV, emphasis mine).

Exodus 19:11 – *"and be ready by the third day, because on that day the* LORD *will come down on Mount Sinai in the sight of all of the people"* (NIV, emphasis mine).

So, let us do a simple calculation from the time they left Egypt until Exodus 19:11. From the fourteenth of Aviv, the first month of the Hebrew calendar, to the end of that month is seventeen days. The next month has thirty days, so by adding thirty to the previous seventeen, we have a sum of forty-seven days.

Then, adding the last three days that are mentioned in Exodus 19:11, we come to a grand total of fifty (50) days. These fifty days will become very important again when we discuss the New Covenant, so remember them.

Now that we are in possession of the total amount of time it took the nation of Israel to get from Egypt to Mount Sinai, let's see what happened when they got there.

Marriage at Mount Sinai

Most people would assume that the most significant event that occurred at Mt. Sinai was the giving of the Ten Commandments—and they would be correct. However, let's look a bit deeper, beyond the surface.

Since we know that this is where the Ten Commandments were given, and that this is a significant event in the life of Israel, we need to ask, "What was the Father doing relationally with Israel?" Mt. Sinai is where the Father used covenant language and set the terms by which He agreed to be their God. But it is much more than that, as this is where Israel, by agreeing to the terms of the covenant, both its rewards and its punishments, entered into a marriage covenant with God. Yes, here at Mt. Sinai is where YHVH married Israel.

The Ten Commandments, and the rest of the Mosaic Law/Torah, became the de-facto *Ketubah*, or Hebrew marriage contract. These were Israel's "Instructions for Life." This is how He wanted them to live and be **holy**, which simply means to be set apart unto Him. To prove this, let us go to Ezekiel, the book of the Bible where YHVH, Himself, recounts entering into His relationship with Israel.

Ezekiel 16:4-9 – *"⁴As for your birth, in the day you were born your navel was not cut, neither were you washed in water to cleanse you; you weren't salted at all, nor swaddled at all. ⁵No eye pitied you, to do any of these things to you, to have compassion on you; but you were cast out in the open field, for that your person was abhorred, in the day that you were born. ⁶When I passed by you, and saw you wallowing in your blood, I said to you, Though you are in your blood, live; yes, I said to you,*

*Though you are in your blood, live. ⁷I caused you to multiply as that which grows in the field, and you increased and grew great, and you attained to excellent ornament; your breasts were fashioned, and your hair was grown; yet you were naked and bare. ⁸Now when I passed by you, and looked at you, behold, **your time was the time of love; and I spread my skirt over you, and covered your nakedness: yes, I swore to you, and entered into a covenant with you, says the Lord Yahweh, and you became mine.** ⁹Then washed I you with water; yes, I thoroughly washed away your blood from you, and I anointed you with oil"* (WEB, emphasis mine).

The picture being painted here in the Scripture above is wonderfully graphic. God commits that He is taking personal responsibility for the creation and life of the nation of Israel. How wonderful is that? He said to Israel in her blood, "Live!" He is so very personal with Israel that later he marries her. Anyone living today that is concerned about the destruction of Israel by her enemies need not be. YHVH, the Father Himself, is personally responsible for her life.

In verse eight, God says that He spread His wing over Israel and covered her nakedness. He swore an oath and entered into a covenant with Israel (this is marriage language), and she became His. He washed off her blood and anointed her with oil. The washing off of the blood is a picture of the blood of a virgin after intercourse. When a virgin is married and has intercourse, her hymen membrane breaks and there is a release of blood. God is personally washing His bride and then anointing her with oil, which is a picture of healing and restoration. The oil is a representation of the Holy Spirit of God. These are all pictures of the Father as a loving husband to His bride, Israel.

Knowing that God actually married Israel at Mt. Sinai becomes supremely important later, because in order for the bride, Old Covenant Israel, to be free from that law (specifically that marriage covenant, the Mosaic Law), the husband, God in the form of Jesus, had to die. Only then could Israel be **free** to marry another, "*...even to him who is raised from the dead*" (Romans 7:3-4).

The Old Covenant Pentecost

Let us return now to Mount Sinai to glean some details of how the Old Covenant compares to the New Covenant instituted by Yeshua.

Once Israel arrived at Mount Sinai, YHVH told Moses that if the people would keep His covenant they would be to Him a kingdom of priests and a holy nation (Exodus 19:6). Interestingly, this is nearly the exact same language that the Father, through Peter the Apostle, used to reference His New Covenant people.

1 Peter 2:9 – *"But you are a chosen race, a royal priesthood, a holy nation, a people for God's own possession..."* (WEB).

Then Moses was instructed to consecrate the people and they were to wash their clothes—again, we see just the outer garments, as this is what the Old Covenant dealt with, the people's outward behavior.

Two noteworthy events happened next. First, God descended upon the mountain in fire and second, in chapter thirty-two, three thousand people died because of the golden calf incident. This is where Aaron and the people fashioned an Apis, a pagan golden calf deity, and declared that it was the god that brought them out of Egypt. They effectively turned their backs on the Father who had done so many miracles for them when they had left Egypt and threw themselves headlong into pagan worship.

Exodus 19:14 & 18 – *"¹⁴Moses went down from the mountain to the people, and sanctified the people; and they washed their clothes... ¹⁸All of Mount Sinai smoked, because Yahweh descended on it in **fire**; and its smoke ascended like **the smoke of a furnace**, and the whole mountain quaked greatly"* (WEB, emphasis mine).

Exodus 20:5 – *"...for I the* LORD *thy God am a jealous God, visiting the iniquity of the fathers upon the children unto the third and fourth generation..."* (KJV).

Exodus 31:18 – *"He gave to Moses, when he finished speaking with him on Mount Sinai, the two tablets of the testimony, stone tablets, written with God's finger"* (WEB).

Exodus 32:19 & 25-26, 28 – *"19It happened, as soon as he came near to the camp, that he saw the calf and the dancing: and Moses' anger grew hot, and he threw the tablets out of his hands, and broke them beneath the mountain...*

25When Moses saw that the people had broken loose, (for Aaron had let them loose for a derision among their enemies), 26then Moses stood in the gate of the camp, and said, "Whoever is on Yahweh's side, come to me!" All the sons of Levi gathered themselves together to him...

28The sons of Levi did according to the word of Moses: and there fell of the people that day about **three thousand men**" (WEB, emphasis mine).

So, to synopsize this part of the Old Covenant: On Passover, the nation of Israel applies the blood of a perfect lamb to the outside of their dwellings. They leave after midnight on the 14th of their first month (effectively the 15th), then leave their slave masters and come out of Egypt, which is representative of the devil's world system. Then, YHVH God comes down on the mountain in fire, and, separately, because of their pagan worship, three thousand men of the Hebrew people die. YHVH then gives His people the Ten Commandments, the Hebrew marriage contract, the *Ketubah*.

These are their instructions for life on how they are to walk in order to be in relationship with YHVH as His people and bride. The Ten Commandments are later written in stone (yes, this is where the phrase comes from) by the finger of YHVH Himself. These tablets of stone are also a composite picture of what this marriage covenant (that Israel agreed to and said they could perform) will require of them, how it will relate to them, and what it will be like, which is:

COLD, HARD, LIFELESS, INFLEXIBLE and MERCILESS.

The Feast Day, or appointed time (in Hebrew *moed*; or Holy appointed times *moedim*), when the Ten Commandments were given is known in Hebrew as *Shavuot,* or the Feast of Weeks. In the New Covenant, this feast day is called PENTECOST!

1 Corinthians 5:7

"For indeed Christ, our Passover, has been sacrificed in our place" (WEB).

Chapter Three
The New Covenant Passover and Pentecost

As the last word of the previous paragraph may have given away, the pictures in the Old Covenant Passover and Pentecost story were going to be repeated again, establishing the New Covenant, approximately 1500 years after the covenant at Mt. Sinai. As we will see, although the pictures of what Jesus did as God's perfect Passover lamb correspond perfectly to what took place in the Old Testament, what this perfect New Covenant Lamb accomplished, and the benefits that were bestowed upon all who believe (Romans 3:22), was far beyond anything the Old Covenant Believers could have dreamed. Let's look at a synopsis of those events and their correlation to the Old Covenant story.

Jesus, as the Lamb of God who took away the sin of the world, was the New Covenant fulfillment of the Old Covenant's ineffective, natural Passover lamb (John 1:29). He would further qualify Himself as the Passover Lamb by being observed for four days, just as the Old Covenant Passover lamb also had to be examined for four days before being declared perfect.

The length of time preceding His crucifixion—from when He entered Jerusalem, to His arrest, being sent from Annas, Caiaphas, Pontius Pilate, Herod, and then again back to Pontius Pilate—was a period of four days. The pagan Roman authority, Pilate, not knowing he was fulfilling the Old Covenant Passover lamb requirement of perfection, after examining Jesus, declared to the chief priests, "*I find no fault in this man*," (Luke 23:4). Jesus, through Pilate's declaration, fulfilled the four-day requirement of the Old Covenant Passover lamb perfectly:

Exodus 12:3, 5-6 – "³...*In the **tenth day of this month** they shall take to them every man a lamb...* **⁵***Your lamb shall be **without blemish**, a male of the first year: ye shall take it out from the sheep, or from the goats:* **⁶***And ye shall keep it up until the **fourteenth day of the same month**...* " (KJV, emphasis mine).

There is absolutely no way that Jesus could have coordinated the events of these four days to happen, since all the other parties involved were vehemently against him. These events were the supernatural fulfillment of age-old prophecies orchestrated by the Father Himself because Jesus had to fulfill these requirements to be Israel's Messiah.

Health and Provision in New Covenant

Later on, we will discuss the provision aspect of the New Covenant, but for now let's look closely at how Jesus provided health for us at the cross. In addition to providing a means to salvation, Jesus went beyond the Old Covenant Passover lamb picture. The natural lamb was mercifully killed and would bleed out after having its throat cut by an expert butcher, a trained Levite. Jesus, on the other hand, endured the most severe and torturous beating that any human has ever borne.

The million-dollar question is, "Why did He to do this?" Why was it not enough for Jesus to simply fulfill the Old Covenant picture of the lamb dying mercifully? Jesus' beating was for a reason! One reason was to fulfill prophecy, but by being beaten

He also gave Believers the legal right to claim physical healing as part of the New Covenant. Yes, physical healing has been purchased for us by our Savior, and here is the proof:

Isaiah 53:4 – *"Surely he hath borne our griefs, and carried our sorrows..."* (KJV).

Isaiah 53:5 – *"...and with his stripes we are healed"* (KJV).

The words "griefs" and "sorrows" are extremely poor translations of the actual Hebrew text. Because of this, the plain, but powerful, meaning of this verse is clouded and lost. The words "griefs" and "sorrows" are so vague in comparison to what the text actually states, that one can only wonder that perhaps the translators thought the actual Hebrew words were too wonderful and did not believe what they were reading.

Because of this mistake, the translators minimized the meanings of the words and consequently minimized the victory that Jesus actually accomplished by taking the scourging stripes—the ones that were rightfully ours.

The word translated "griefs" is the Hebrew word *choli*. *Choli* is Strong's Concordance word #2483, and it is translated "sickness."

The word translated "sorrows" is the Hebrew word *makob,* or *makov*. This is Strong's Concordance word #4341 and it is translated "pains."

So, the Scripture should actually read, "Surely he hath borne our sicknesses and our pains..."

The secondary point you should see is that in no way can this be interpreted as some type of spiritual healing: it is actual physical sicknesses and pains!

The second Scripture, Isaiah 53:5, reveals the means by which our healing was put into effect, *"...and with his stripes we are healed."*

What adds even more weight to this Scripture is that it is quoted subsequently, and in the **past tense**, by the Apostle Peter after Jesus died. Peter was obviously looking back to something that had already been accomplished.

1 Peter 2:24 – *"Who Himself bore our sins in His own body on the tree, that we, having died to sins, might live for righteousness—by whose stripes you* ***were*** *healed"* (NKJV, emphasis mine).

The natural question after reading the Hebrew translation of these words is the following: Why then, are not all Believers healed? Since healing is part of the atonement, and one of the promises of God, why has it not manifested for every Believer?

Additional questions came to me years ago, while traveling in Russia with Charles and Frances Hunter, known as "The Healing Hunters." I witnessed non-Believers receive their healing! Since I witnessed this happen, my internal question was, "Why are not all Believers automatically healed, since Believers are part of the family of the New Covenant?"

Although I do not have a 'hard and fast' answer for these, let us at least elucidate some of the reasons. First of all, praise God that He often uses healing and miracles as a "dinner bell" for the unsaved, in order to get them saved. Second, the sad reality is this: not all Believers have even read Isaiah 53:4, or if they have, they may have over spiritualized it, and believed that it is talking about our spiritual healing—our salvation.

Third, if they have read it, they may not have looked up the correct translation that I have just detailed for you above. We know that faith comes by hearing, and hearing by the Word of God (Romans 10:17). But if you are not reading and hearing what the Scripture is actually saying, you are, at a disadvantage and not getting the full picture and benefit of the Scripture in which you are putting your faith.

So, part of the answer is, just like salvation, healing is about appropriating the promise. In other words, you must know you have the promise and then agree with and accept the promise. In fact, you may have to believe the promise in the Father's Word in the face of evidence in your body to the contrary. I am **not** saying, however, to just do something because of something you have read in Scripture. You must know that faith has come and follow the leading of the Holy Spirit.

Also, another possibility for why all Believers are not healed is because healing in our bodies is in the physical realm, not exclusively in the spiritual realm as is salvation, though both originate there. What I mean is this: Once you say you accept Jesus, and give your heart to Him, the devil cannot stop your salvation. The nanosecond you said, "Yes," it was already done.

Healing, on the other hand, manifests in the physical realm, in our bodies and souls (minds, wills, and emotions). We can mentally understand the Scriptures, but because of how we were raised, or things that have happened in our lives, we may have difficulty accepting them. Our adversary may also use circumstances or symptoms to get us into doubt and unbelief. Every one of us is on our own separate walk with the Lord, so healing may come differently for each of us. It may even be that as you minister the **truth** of healing (that it is part of Jesus' atonement) to someone else, that you yourself may be healed.

The Apostle Peter states that we are to "...*grow in the grace and knowledge of our Lord and Savior Jesus Christ*" (2 Peter 3:18). My point in detailing these Scriptures is to simply reveal the truth of the Word of God, which is that healing has been paid for, and is available, because of what Jesus has done. We have been healed by the stripes of Jesus and by His atonement.

Paul recounts Jesus' own words in 1 Corinthians 11:24. *"This is my body which is broken for you."* Start with this truth, that healing is already yours, and as a little child go on from there to receive your healing!

My own miracle happened over fifteen years after my dad had dropped a tractor scoop on my foot, when I was twelve years old. My right foot, as an adult, was approximately a half inch shorter than my left one. One night in Dallas, on June 7th, 1988, a healing evangelist prayed over my foot and I saw it grow out before my own eyes! I drew outlines of my feet the day before the miracle happened, showing the right foot being smaller than the left, so that I could prove it. That was the level and strength of my faith that day, as I knew that my foot was going to be healed that night.

My particular miracle was technically outside of the strict healing definition of "sickness and pain," but it happened just the same, to make me whole. This is part of what the Hebrew word *Shalom* means: wholeness in all things. So, DO NOT LIMIT GOD. He is your good Father, Jesus is the Good Shepherd, and He is going to do mighty works in these last days. Your healing has already been accomplished by Jesus!

Back to Our Passover Picture

After Jesus' death, instead of physically applying the blood of a natural lamb to the outside of our dwellings, New Testament Believers in Jesus apply His blood to the inside of our dwellings. Remember, the Old Covenant only dealt with a person's outside/outward actions, not their hearts or spirits. So, by repenting and asking Jesus to cleanse us spiritually, we apply the cleansing blood of God's Lamb to our spirits, which is the inside of our dwelling, as His perfect blood washes away our sins forever and changes our hearts. This act of faith, of all who will humble themselves, restores our spirits back into union with the Spirit of God the Father, making our spirits perfect.

1 Corinthians 5:7 – *"...For even Christ our passover is sacrificed for us"* (KJV).

John 14:6-7 – *"⁶Jesus saith unto him, I am the way, the truth, and the life: no man cometh unto the Father, but by me. ⁷If ye had known me, ye should have known my Father also: and from henceforth ye know him, and have seen him""* (KJV).

1 Corinthians 6:17 – *"But he who is joined to the Lord is one spirit"* (WEB).

Hebrews 12:23 – *"...to the spirits of just men made perfect"* (WEB).

Believers in the New Covenant that God has made with man through Jesus, His only begotten Son, also go through a baptism by water as Old Covenant Israel did. The New Covenant baptism signifies the death of the old nature, as the believer is immersed in the water. Then, the coming up out of the water signifies the newness of life.

Romans 6:4-6 – *"⁴Therefore we are buried with him by baptism into death: that like as Christ was raised up from the dead by the glory of the Father, even so we also should walk in newness of life. ⁵For if we have been planted together in the likeness of his death, we shall be also in the likeness of his resurrection: ⁶Knowing this, that our old man is crucified with him, that the body of sin might be destroyed, that henceforth we should not serve sin"* (KJV).

This completes the picture of the New Covenant Passover. Now let's move on to the picture of the New Covenant Pentecost.

The New Covenant Fifty Days

After Jesus' crucifixion, the apostles were despondent because, in their minds, Jesus had fallen short of what they wanted Him to do, which was to restore the kingdom of Israel (Acts 1:6). However, after His resurrection Jesus appeared to the apostles several times over the course of forty days.

Acts 1:3 – *"...To whom he also shewed himself alive after his passion by many infallible proofs, being seen of them forty days, and speaking of the things pertaining to the kingdom of God."*

During His last appearance to them, Jesus instructed them to wait in Jerusalem for the Holy Spirit to be poured out, as He had promised them.

Acts 1:4-5 & 8-11 – "*4And, being assembled together with them, commanded them that they should not depart from Jerusalem, but wait for the promise of the Father, which, saith he, ye have heard of me. 5For John truly baptized with water; but ye shall be baptized with the Holy Ghost not many days hence...*

*8But **ye shall receive POWER, after that the Holy Ghost is come upon you:** and ye shall be witnesses unto me both in Jerusalem, and in all Judea, and in Samaria, and unto the uttermost part of the earth. 9And when he had spoken these things, while they beheld, he was taken up; and a cloud received him out of their sight. 10And while they looked steadfastly toward heaven as he went up, behold, two men stood by them in white apparel; 11Which also said, Ye men of Galilee, why stand ye gazing up into heaven? this same Jesus, which is taken up from you into heaven, shall so come in like manner as ye have seen him go into heaven*" (KJV, emphasis mine).

Yes, He IS coming back again, Halleluyah!

Then, a mere 10 days later (for a total of fifty days), on the Hebrew Feast of *Shavuot* (New Covenant Pentecost), came an event that had never happened before. It actually could not have happened, had Jesus not died, and rose again, to take away the sin of the world, because prior to that, man still bore the sin of Adam. On the day of Pentecost, on Mount Zion, the God of the universe poured out His Holy Spirit, the Spirit of His Son, upon man, and the world would never again be the same.

Acts 2:1-3 – "*1And in the day of Pentecost being fulfilled, they were all with one accord at the same place, 2and there came suddenly out of the heaven a sound as of a bearing violent breath, and it filled all the house where they were sitting, 3and there appeared to them **divided tongues, as it were of fire; it sat also upon each one of them**"* (Young's Literal Translation, emphasis mine).

Later in this same chapter, God chose Peter Bar Jonah to deliver a rousing speech about this outpouring of the Holy Spirit (see also Matthew 16:17). Interestingly, in Hebrew his name means Son of the Dove, and the dove is a symbol for the Holy Spirit. So, the Father, in His awesomeness, chose a man whose name means son of the dove to give the introductory speech for the outpouring of the Dove!

Toward the end of Peter's Pentecost speech, a positive supernatural event takes place at Mt. Zion that correlates to the negative one at Mt. Sinai. The Old Covenant event is where 3000 people died after the giving of the Mosaic Law at Mt. Sinai. The New Covenant event is detailed below by Peter:

Acts 2:39-41 – *"³⁹For the promise is unto you, and to your children, and to all that are afar off, even as many as the Lord our God shall call. ⁴⁰And with many other words did he testify and exhort, saying, Save yourselves from this untoward generation. ⁴¹Then they that gladly received his word were baptized: and the same day there were added unto them about three thousand souls"* (KJV, emphasis mine).

What a stark picture and comparison of the covenants: At the inauguration of the Old Covenant, 3000 people died (Exodus 32:28), but at the inauguration of the New Covenant, 3000 people received eternal life! The numbers are the same, but the results are exactly opposite.

This difference in results is at the heart of these two covenants. One brings life, and the other brings death! Also, remember in the Old Covenant God said He would remember, or "visit" the sins of the father to the third and fourth generation (Exodus 20:5). However, in the New Covenant He stated, *"For I will be merciful to their unrighteousness, and their sins and their iniquities will I remember no more"* (Hebrews 8:12).

New Covenant Pentecost

So far, we have seen how Jesus is a perfect picture of the Passover Lamb and how the New Covenant water baptism and the fifty days from Passover to Pentecost correlate perfectly to the events in the Old Covenant. Having seen that, can there be any doubt that the remainder of the New Covenant events will correlate with the Old Covenant events from nearly 1500 years earlier? Let's check it out by looking at three other comparisons.

Mount Zion

First, although the people of God in the New Testament are not physically at Mount Sinai, as they were in the Old Covenant, they are on Mount Zion, another name for Jerusalem. Therefore, as they are on a mountain, there is a perfect correlation to the Old Covenant picture of the event that also took place on a mountain.

It is also not surprising, and altogether appropriate, that these first people (who typify all Believers who come after them) to-receive this empowering gift would specifically be on Mount Zion, as there is a hidden meaning in the name itself. The word "Mount," can be seen in Scripture as a spiritual picture for "kingdom," or "authority," as in the Scriptures below:

Zechariah 4:7 – *"Who art thou, O great mountain? before Zerubbabel thou shalt become a plain: and he shall bring forth the headstone thereof with shoutings, crying, Grace, grace unto it"* (KJV).

Mark 11:23 – *"For verily I say unto you, That whosoever shall say unto this mountain, Be thou removed, and be thou cast into the sea; and shall not doubt in his heart, but shall believe that those things which he saith shall come to pass; he shall have whatsoever he saith"* (KJV).

So, the word "mount," or "mountain," can be, metaphorically, seen in Scripture as an authority or kingdom!

Also, a friend of mine, Rami Danieli, a Messianic Jew living in Israel, confirmed with me that the word "ZION" (in Hebrew, *Tziyon*) is connected with another Hebrew word, *Tziun*, which means "marker, marked, or marking." In essence, these people would be "marked," or be "distinctive." If you tie the two words together—Mount and Zion—we would say that they have a "marked, or distinctive, Kingdom" from the Father. The disciples who have received this baptism of the Holy Spirit would also be "marked" because of having power (gifts) from the Holy Spirit (Ephesians 4:8).

1 Corinthians 4:20 – *"For the kingdom of God is not in word, but in power"* (KJV).

1 Corinthians 12:7-10 – *"7But the manifestation of the Spirit is given to every man to profit withal. 8For to one is given by the Spirit the word of wisdom; to another the word of knowledge by the same Spirit; 9To another faith by the same Spirit; to another the gifts of healing by the same Spirit; 10To another the working of miracles; to another prophecy; to another discerning of spirits; to another divers kinds of tongues; to another the interpretation of tongues"* (KJV).

Unfortunately, we are not seeing this power in the Body of Christ today because many Believers have either operated in the gifts of the Spirit in disorder, or they have denied them altogether.

From the words of Jesus, we are given insight to another marked, or distinctive, quality of the Believers in Jesus and the New Covenant:

John 13:35 – *"By this shall all men know that ye are my disciples, if ye have love one to another"* (KJV).

This love is not a love that originates from the mind or heart of un-regenerated man. This is a love that has never been seen on Earth before; this is *agape* love. This is a supernatural love that comes from being filled with the Holy Spirit of God.

The Fire of God

Secondly, regarding the Feast of Pentecost, you will remember that YHVH came down on Mount Sinai in fire. In the New Covenant, the Father once again came down on a mountain, Mount Zion, in fire—tongues of fire. However, this time God is much more personal in His approach, just as this covenant is more personal in all aspects. This time, the fire of God rests upon individual Believers.

So, while I have been pointing out the many similarities between the two covenants, I hope you have also seen the overarching difference: The New Covenant, that Jesus made for us with the Father, is not about religion (bondage), **but about relationship**. And this relationship is very personal.

During Pentecost, God comes down and rests His Holy Spirit upon each New Covenant Believer, individually. This is a very personal and intimate act by the Father, who is a personal God to each of His people. This can be easily overlooked when reading the Scripture narrative.

Acts 2:1-4 – "*¹And when the day of Pentecost was fully come, they were all with one accord in one place. ²And suddenly there came a sound from heaven as of a rushing mighty wind, and it filled all the house where they were sitting, ³And there appeared unto them cloven tongues like as of fire, and it **sat upon each of them.** ⁴And they were all filled with the Holy Ghost, and began to speak with other tongues, as the Spirit gave them utterance*" (KJV, emphasis mine).

This radical concept, that YHVH is a personal God, who wants to make a way for all of mankind to know Him personally through His Son, Jesus, is unique among all beliefs systems in the world. So, let's examine the very personal, and spiritual, meaning of the tongues of fire.

The Hebrew Letter SHIN – God's Symbol

One of the most amazing pieces of Hebrew understanding that my wife, Vicki, and I acquired during our ten years living under the Torah, was the meaning of the Hebrew letter *shin*. As mentioned earlier, the Hebrew alphabet, or aleph-bet, has twenty-two letters. Each letter also represents a number, each number has a meaning, and each letter has a corresponding pictogram, or picture.

The letter *shin* occupies the twenty-first position in the Hebrew aleph-bet. Twenty-one is the number 7 times 3. Seven is the number of completion or perfection, and three means divine or resurrection. Put another way, *shin* is the number seven, appearing three times.

Since the number 7 means perfection, it can be stated that the letter *shin* is (7 + 7 + 7), because YHVH is a thrice Holy God. There are three members of the Godhead, Father, Son and Holy Spirit, each who are Holy. In fact, it is often written this way in Scripture with the phrase, "Holy, Holy, Holy is the LORD."

Separately, a Hebrew word study will show you that the numerical value of the letter *shin* is three-hundred, and the meaning of the number three-hundred is **victory**! Finally, the pictogram for *shin* is that of fire or flames.

As you can see, the letter *shin* looks like a flame. This letter is also the single letter from the Hebrew aleph-bet that is used by Jews throughout the world to convey the name, or the main

character of the personage, of YHVH. This is because *shin* is the first letter in *Shaddai*, as in *El Shaddai*, or God Almighty. The *shin* is so meaningful to Jews that it is inscribed on the outside of every *mezuzah* that is attached to the door frame of an observant Jew's home, and kissed upon entry and exit.[2]

---

[2] The *mezuzah* is a small case that typically contains a parchment scroll with the Torah verses Deuteronomy 6:4-9 and Deuteronomy 11:13-21, affirming that God is One, and the promise of His blessings if they are obedient.

The *Shin's* Spiritual Significance

The Father is so loving toward us that on Pentecost, He used the one letter that represents His name and rested it upon each person in attendance. The Father personally and boldly affirmed His love to each one of them by putting the symbol for His name, the *shin*, on them. This symbol says, "YOU are mine, and YOU are mine, and YOU are mine!" And because the number that is represented by shin (300) means victory, He is further saying we are all destined for victory. You, as a Believer and part of the Body of Christ, are made for victory in this covenant, because **Jesus**, the originator and mediator of this New Covenant, has won the victory over sin, death and the devil!

Galatians 4:7 – *"Wherefore thou art no more a servant, but a son; and if a son, then an heir of God through Christ"* (KJV).

I think that deserves a Halleluyah!

In Hebrew, *hallel* means praise, and *yah* is a shortened version of *Yahweh*, so Halleluyah means "Praise Yahweh!"

The Holy Spirit and the Believer

At this point, I would like to address a teaching that is in the Body of Christ regarding the baptism of the Holy Spirit. There are those in the Body of Christ that argue that the Holy Spirit baptism was **only** poured out on those in attendance at Pentecost, or that this experience was only for the first century church.

These Believers defend this position with the observation that during the first century outpouring on Pentecost, these "tongues of fire," came from Heaven and rested on the heads of the Believers. Today, when people receive the baptism of the Holy Spirit, this sign is not seen. Therefore, they hold the position that the modern-day Holy Spirit baptism experience cannot be authentic.

Therefore, many believe that the baptism in the Holy Spirit and the gifts of the Holy Spirit are invalid for today. In essence, they believe that everything that happens to Believers happens when we are born again. They further state that the languages that accompanied the outpouring of the Holy Spirit on Pentecost were understandable by at least part of those in attendance, but the languages that accompany the experience today are typically not understandable. To them, this further invalidates the baptism of the Holy Spirit today.

My first point would be to point out that Scripture indicates that there are at least two baptisms, and that they are carried out by different persons. We see in 1 Corinthians 12:13 that it is the Holy Spirit that baptizes us into the Body of Christ. (To be born again means you are part of Jesus' Body on Earth, since He has ascended into Heaven.)

1 Corinthians 12:13 – *"For by one Spirit are we all baptized into one body, whether we be Jews or Gentiles…"* (KJV).

However, it is Jesus who baptizes us with the Holy Spirit.

John 1:33 – *"I didn't recognize him, but he who sent me to baptize in water, he said to me, 'On whomever you will see the Spirit descending, and remaining on him, the same is he who baptizes in the Holy Spirit'"* (WEB).

These two Scriptures make it clear that these are two separate and distinctive events.

In addition, depending on your upbringing, you may maintain that this empowerment was only for the first century church and has since vanished, or that everything spiritually happens when you are born again. Let me see if I can shed light on why the circumstances above are what they are by going to the Word of God.

Let's begin by agreeing that all Believers are part of a royal priesthood and (each of us individually) are the temple of the Holy Spirit. Therefore, even if you have not experienced the baptism of the Holy Spirit, in the Father's eyes you are not "less" than anybody who has, and anybody who has is not "more." This is not about exclusivity, but about all of us inheriting everything that Jesus paid for.

1 Peter 2:9 – *"But ye are a chosen generation, **a royal priesthood, an holy nation**, a peculiar people; that ye should shew forth the praises of him who hath called you out of darkness into his marvelous light"* (KJV, emphasis mine).

1 Corinthians 3:16 – *"Know ye not that **ye are the temple of God**, and that the Spirit of God dwelleth in you?"* (KJV, emphasis mine).

1 Corinthians 6:19 – *"What? know ye not **that your body is the temple of the Holy Ghost which is in you,** which ye have of God, and ye are not your own?"* (KJV, emphasis mine).

You may also be asking the question, "Why is there not any fire falling from Heaven today?" The answer is found in the three temples established by the Father.

The First Temple

First, we begin by peeling apart the pages of the Book of Leviticus chapter eight. In this chapter, God had Moses set Aaron and his sons apart as priests and anointed them. Later, in chapter nine, Moses and Aaron prepared to dedicate the, "Temple in the Wilderness." Aaron offered the sin offering, the burnt offering and the peace offerings on the altar.

Leviticus 9:23-24 – *"23And Moses and Aaron went into the tabernacle of the congregation, and came out, and blessed the people: and the glory of the LORD appeared unto all the people. 24And there came **a fire out from before the LORD**, and consumed upon the altar the burnt offering and the fat: which when all the people saw, they shouted, and fell on their faces"* (KJV, emphasis mine).

Leviticus 6:13 – *"A fire shall always be burning on the altar; it shall never go out"* (NKJV).

And so, we see a picture: the priests of the Lord are set in office, and while God started the fire on the altar from Heaven, it was up to man, the priests, to fan the flame and keep it burning.

The Second Temple

Next, let's refer to the book of 2 Chronicles, where we find the account of King Solomon and the dedication of the temple that he had built for God.

2 Chronicles 7:1 – *"When Solomon had finished praying, fire came down from heaven and consumed the burnt offering and the sacrifices; and the glory of the* LORD *filled the temple"* (NKJV).

Here again, we see the same picture. The Father again sent fire from Heaven down upon the altar to consume the sacrifice. However, going forward, it was be up to the priests to maintain the fire. The priesthood had already been set apart for service, in Leviticus chapter eight, so there was no need to anoint any priests.

The Third Temple

The third temple is comprised of all Believers in Jesus:

1 Corinthians 3:16 – *"Know ye not that **ye are the temple of God**, and that the Spirit of God dwelleth in you"* (KJV).

1 Corinthians 6:19 – *"What? know ye not **that your body is the temple of the Holy Ghost which is in you**, which ye have of God, and ye are not your own"* (KJV).

On Pentecost, the Father dedicated His New Covenant Temple(s) by outpouring His Holy Spirit fire down upon His designated temple(s): The Believers in Jesus who gathered in one place and in one accord.

But wait, where are the sacrifices? There are no sacrifices at this New Covenant temple dedication for this Holy Fire to consume, as there had been at the other two temples. The perfect sacrifice for the New Covenant temple(s) had already been made by Jesus' death (and resurrection) during the Passover Feast fifty days before Pentecost.

There is also an additional picture that we as Believers, need to see. When God's fire came down from Heaven on the sacrifices in the Old Covenant temples, this fire *consumed* the sacrifices. So, the judgment was greater than the sacrifices. However, in the New Covenant, when the judgment of God for our sins was placed upon Jesus at the cross, the sacrifice remained. The sacrifice, Jesus, the Son of God, was greater than the judgment.

Jesus is greater than all our sins—past, present and future!

So, the answer to the question, "Why don't we see tongues of fire today when someone gets baptized in the Holy Spirit?" is because this New Covenant event is following the Old Covenant pattern established by God twice before. *The Father starts the fire*, but it has always been up to man to maintain it.

Is the picture of this pattern of man maintaining God's fire discussed anywhere in the New Testament? Yes, in fact, this is exactly what the Apostle Paul encouraged his son in the faith, Timothy, to do.

2 Timothy 1:6 – *"For this reason I remind you to fan into flame the gift of God, which is in you through the laying on of my hands"* (NKJV).

The Languages

Besides the three temples, the second issue is the one regarding the languages heard at Pentecost, so let us turn our attention there. Why, in most cases, are the languages of people receiving the baptism of the Holy Spirit not understood? First of all, if you look closely, the Scripture does not say that those speaking in other "tongues" were speaking in other languages, but rather that the bystanders, all from foreign lands, *heard* what was spoken in their own languages. Those baptized in the Holy Spirit were *speaking* in other tongues, yet those in attendance *heard* them in their native languages.

Simply put, what happened on Pentecost was for the people that were there. In this particular instance at the initial outpouring, they understood it in their own languages. However, Paul later stated that this would not always be the case.

Paul expands on the issue of other tongues, whether by initial baptism of the Holy Spirit or as a gift of the Spirit, rather simply in 1 Corinthians 14:2. In 1 Corinthians 14:2, the Apostle Paul, referencing tongues, gives an additional reason why the language will not be understood.

1 Corinthians 14:2 – *"For he who speaks in another language speaks not to men, but to God; for no one understands; but in the Spirit he speaks mysteries"* (WEB).

Paul is specifically stating that when someone speaks in an unknown tongue, they are not speaking to men, but to God, and no man understands it. He ends by stating that in the Spirit he speaks mysteries. Someone speaking in tongues is speaking mysteries. These mysteries are defined in the Interlinear Bible as *"the counsels of God."* He is speaking things, out of his union with the Holy Spirit, that he does not know in his natural mind.

Death vs Life

The third and final point in making our comparison and contrast of the New Covenant events to the Old Covenant events, is one that I have mentioned earlier.

So that no mistake could be made between the Old Covenant and the New Covenant, the Father makes a (non-verbal, yet powerful) statement contrasting the two covenants: The Old Covenant brings death and the New Covenant brings life (Romans 5:17-19).

Remember, shortly after the inauguration of the Old Covenant, after the Mosaic Law was given, three thousand people died (Exodus 32:28), but at the inauguration of the New Covenant, three thousand people received eternal life (Acts 2:41)! So, the picture we see corresponds perfectly, it is just that the results were directly opposite.

One covenant brought death and the other brought life. And the New Covenant offer is available not only to those that were there, but to all who accept Jesus in the future. Peter, referencing the offer of salvation and the baptism of the Holy Spirit, makes the following promise from God:

Acts 2:39 – *"For the promise is unto you, and to your children, and to all that are afar off, even as many as the Lord our God shall call"* (KJV).

Now, if you are not a born-again Believer (who trusts in Jesus, and His blood, for forgiveness of sins), there is another side of the New Covenant coin. If you wish to be righteous before God independent of Jesus' sacrifice—regardless of what church you belong to, despite all the good deeds you have done, all the poor you have helped, or all the money you have given—you are duty bound to obey ALL of the Mosaic Law, ALL of the time: in thought, in word and in deed!

After trying to follow the Mosaic Law myself for a decade, I can offer you just four words of encouragement:

GOOD LUCK WITH THAT!

You will discover it is a game you cannot win!

Summary

Now, let us look at the "whole ball of wax": we have seen in these pictures, that because of New Covenant events, the Mosaic Law has been fulfilled by Jesus, and therefore is no longer for the righteous Believer.

1 Timothy 1:9 – *"Knowing this, that the law is not made for a righteous man, but for the lawless and disobedient, for the ungodly and for sinners..."* (KJV).

The reason it is for sinners, not Believers, is because the purpose of the Mosaic Law is to show you that you can't do it. You cannot successfully perform the Mosaic Law for your salvation or for your holiness on your own. When you realize this fact, you will be driven to Jesus and be changed from the inside out as His blood makes your spirit perfect and in union with Father God.

As mentioned earlier, Jesus, God's perfect lamb, just like the Old Covenant Passover lamb, had to be declared perfect. Jesus came into Jerusalem before Passover and was examined for four days, just like the Old Covenant lamb. He had lived a perfect, blameless life in view of all Israel. No one had been able to bring a legitimate accusation against Him. After being examined by the authorities, both religious (Annas and Caiaphas) and civil (Herod and Pontius Pilate), He was pronounced perfect by Pilate, the Roman Governor, when he said, *"I find no fault in him,"* (Luke 23:4).

Interestingly, Pilate used the word "in" him, versus the more commonly used judicial word "with" him. Not that Pilate knew the significance of what he was saying, but he was speaking more truth than he realized. Not only had Jesus not done, nor spoken, any wrong, but He had thought no wrong either. There was no sin in Him.

Indeed, according to Jesus' own words, even the prince of this world, the devil, could find no darkness in Him.

John 14:30 – *"Hereafter I will not talk much with you: for the prince of this world cometh, and hath nothing in me"* (KJV).

After He was crucified, Jesus dismissed His Spirit of His own free will. He said, *"No man taketh it from me, but I lay it down of myself,"* (John 10:18) and His blood was spilled on the earth, redeeming it.

First century followers of Jesus accepted His sacrifice by applying His blood spiritually to the inside of their dwellings, their hearts, protecting them forever from spiritual death, and they are baptized. They are now reconciled to the Father and **saved**!

Acts 16:30-31 – *"³⁰And brought them out, and said, Sirs, what must I do to be saved? ³¹And they said, Believe on the Lord Jesus Christ, and thou shalt be saved, and thy house"* (KJV).

In the Old Covenant, during the first Passover in Egypt, the blood of a perfect lamb was applied to the outside of the Hebrew dwellings. Remember, this is a picture that this covenant only deals with a person's outward behavior. Everyone who applied the blood was protected from the death angel and natural death. They were literally saved!

The children of Israel, led by Moses, then left Egypt the next day, and go through a type of baptism by passing through the Red Sea. Then, after fifty days, on the very first Pentecost, they ended up at Mount Sinai. At Sinai, God came down on the mountain in fire and gave the nation of Israel His *Ketubah*, His marriage contract (Ezekiel 16:8-9), The Ten Commandments, and the complete Mosaic Law. The people agreed to the terms of the covenant.

Exodus 19:8 – *"All the people answered together, and said, "All that Yahweh has spoken we will do." Moses reported the words of the people to Yahweh"* (WEB).

However, after Moses came down from Mount Sinai, before he could even make it down the mountain with the tablets, the people turned their back on YHVH, their God, and went into idolatry. Because of their rebellion, three thousand people died!

In the New Covenant, after Passover, Jesus told His disciples not to leave Jerusalem, as they had not received their power yet through the baptism of the Holy Spirit. They were to wait for the Promise of the Father, the Holy Spirit. Fifty days later, the same time duration as in the Old Covenant, the Holy Spirit

70

was poured out on Believers on Mount Zion (another mountain) with tongues of fire (a picture of the Hebrew letter *shin*, that represents the Father, Himself) that the Father personally put on each Believer. Soon after, three thousand people received eternal life!

In the next chapter we will reveal another picture, hidden in plain sight for two thousand years, showing why the Mosaic Law, including the Ten Commandments, is not for the Body of Christ.

Galatians 5:1

"Christ has set us free in freedom; stand fast therefore, and be not held again in a yoke of bondage" (DBY).

Chapter Four
The Second Picture That No One Has Seen

N o Christian would argue that Jesus, by doing all He did in establishing the New Covenant, fulfilled the Passover Lamb requirements of the Old Covenant (1 Corinthians 5:7). That is to say, Christians do not sacrifice lambs on Passover, because they realize that Jesus fulfilled the Old Covenant and its Passover requirement.

However, most do not see the fulfillment of the second picture that I am about to show you and will argue vehemently that following the Ten Commandments contained in the Mosaic Law is still something we should do for our holiness and sanctification. So, why are the Ten Commandments not for Believers?

Because, just as Jesus has fulfilled the Old Covenant Passover, the Holy Spirit has fulfilled the Old Covenant Pentecost and the need for the Mosaic Law that was given at Sinai. This is the second picture: The Holy Spirit living in you has fulfilled the purpose of the Mosaic Law for Believers—all of the Mosaic Law, even the Ten Commandments.

Old Covenant

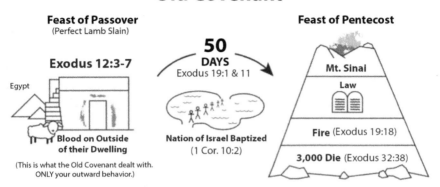

Feast of Passover
(Perfect Lamb Slain)

Exodus 12:3-7

Egypt

Blood on Outside of their Dwelling

(This is what the Old Covenant dealt with. ONLY your outward behavior.)

50 DAYS
Exodus 19:1 & 11

Nation of Israel Baptized
(1 Cor. 10:2)

Feast of Pentecost

Mt. Sinai

Law

Fire (Exodus 19:18)

3,000 Die (Exodus 32:38)

New Covenant

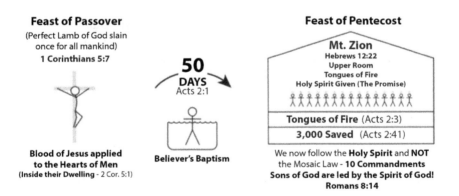

Feast of Passover
(Perfect Lamb of God slain once for all mankind)
1 Corinthians 5:7

Blood of Jesus applied to the Hearts of Men
(Inside their Dwelling - 2 Cor. 5:1)

50 DAYS
Acts 2:1

Believer's Baptism

Feast of Pentecost

Mt. Zion
Hebrews 12:22
Upper Room
Tongues of Fire
Holy Spirit Given (The Promise)

Tongues of Fire (Acts 2:3)

3,000 Saved (Acts 2:41)

We now follow the **Holy Spirit** and **NOT** the Mosaic Law - **10 Commandments**
Sons of God are led by the Spirit of God!
Romans 8:14

Just as Jesus has replaced the Old Covenant Lamb (i.e. we no longer sacrifice lambs), The Holy Spirit has replaced the Mosaic Law for the Believer!

In fact, once you understand the picture, you could explain it in reverse. In other words, you soon realize that if the Holy Spirit being poured out on Pentecost did not completely fulfill the need for the Mosaic Law, then neither has Jesus fulfilled the Old Covenant Passover and we are still dead in our sins (1 Corinthians 15:17). That would not be good news, would it? But, the reality is, you cannot have one without the other. Jesus has fulfilled the Old Covenant Passover lamb and the Holy Spirit has replaced the Mosaic Law for the Believer.

So, as I said near the beginning of the book, it is not that the holiness of YHVH, the Father in Heaven, has been diminished. Nor is it that His righteousness requires anything less than He did under the Mosaic Law. God still requires perfection. But do not be dismayed, because what has changed is the means to that righteousness and perfection of spirit.

We no longer seek God's righteousness through our efforts and the 613 requirements of the Torah. Our righteousness is now found in Jesus alone. Anything added to this is not the Gospel of Jesus Christ. So, instead of being frustrated by trying to perform any part of the Mosaic Law, the whole world needs to realize that through placing our faith in the finished work of Jesus, we are made righteous separate from works of the Mosaic Law (Romans 3:21).

After that step of faith, you now desire to obey the One you have given your heart to and whose Spirit is in you. You have been adopted into His family as a son or daughter, and when you sin, after being adopted, you do not lose your salvation or get un-adopted. When you fall (or sin) you fall IN CHRIST.

This is exactly the same picture that we see with Noah and his family, as they are a picture of God's righteousness during the time that they lived. Scripture states that Noah found grace in the eyes of the LORD (Genesis 6:8). In the same way, all Believers have found grace, a picture of Jesus (John 1:17), in the sight of the Lord. Noah and His family were righteous because they found grace.

The Ark also represents Jesus and salvation, as Noah and his family all took refuge and were found safely in the Ark (in Christ) when judgment came on the earth. They were saved because they were in Christ—the Ark. And if Noah and his family ever fell (sinned), they fell in the Ark.

It is the same for us, when we sin, we fall in Christ. Our salvation and our time on this earth are all about Jesus' finished work and letting His finished work, and His grace, work in you! It is not about you working for His grace; His supply is there.

Now, even though the gift of salvation is free, there is also a heresy being taught that because of Jesus' finished work that "all roads lead to Rome." It, in essence, teaches that everyone will be saved, or is already saved and they just don't know it, and that hell is only a temporary place of purification or a state of mind. This is Universalism and is an incorrect and deadly doctrine. Do not forget, we are all free moral agents, endowed with the power of choice from our Father. We must all choose salvation and who we will follow as God.

More Grace

Part of the good news of the Gospel, is that God's righteousness is the Believer's starting point with Jesus, and holiness in our walk on this earth is achieved the same way we got saved: by grace through faith (Ephesians 2:8).

Many Christians errantly believe that although we are saved by grace, we must practice the Mosaic Law, or at least the Ten Commandments (they seem to neglect the other 603 laws), for holiness while we are here on this earth. This is a deception that puts our eyes back on ourselves, and leads back to the Mosaic Law, which is about self-performance and self-righteousness.

Haven't you had enough of that trap? We need to lift up Jesus and remember that it was His grace that saved us, and it is His grace that will also make us holy in our daily lives. My wife and I have spent most of our adult lives in Texas, and down there we have a country saying, that appropriately explains my point:

"You need to dance with the one that brung ya'."

Since Jesus and His grace "brung" us to the "grace dance" of salvation, we need to continue to dance with Jesus, by trusting Jesus, and His grace for our conduct (our holiness) after we are saved. Grace brought you to Jesus, and grace keeps you walking with Jesus after you are saved, not your natural, self-effort to religious commandments—whether they be ten or six hundred and thirteen.

Jesus did not die and fulfill the Mosaic Law just for you to try and perform it once you have been saved.

Romans 3:21-24 – *"21But now **the righteousness of God without the law** is manifested, being witnessed by the law and the prophets; 22Even **the righteousness of God which is by faith of Jesus Christ unto all and upon all them that believe:** for there is no difference: 23For all have sinned, and come short of the glory of God; 24Being **justified freely by his grace through the redemption that is in Christ Jesus"** (KJV, emphasis mine).

Let's look at these covenants in another way.

In the Old Covenant, God simply could not live inside man because of man's sin nature from Adam, so God had to outline His rules and protections for man. Yes, the Mosaic Law was also for man's protection.

Galatians 3:23-24 – *"23But before faith came, we were guarded under law, shut up to faith [which was] about to be revealed. 24So that the law has been our tutor up to Christ, that we might be justified on the principle of faith"* (Darby Bible Translation).

A simple example from everyday life would be that of a painter in your home. You can't just tell someone to come to your home and paint a room. They have got to know which room, which color, and what type of paint. You tell them, "Here's the paint, here's the brush and drop cloth, and here's how I want you to clean up." You tell them everything because they do not know you as a family member would. This is a picture of the Old Covenant.

Now, however, because of Jesus, you have the One true and living God of the universe living inside you, and you no longer need a set of rules or instructions to tell you what to do. You have been redeemed from the Mosaic Law so that you could be adopted as sons and live your life by His Spirit.

Let me clarify that, when I say that the Holy Spirit replaces the Mosaic Law in our lives, I am not negating the need to study the Word of God. The Scripture, 2 Timothy 3:16 states, "*all scripture is given by inspiration of God, and is profitable for doctrine, for reproof, for correction, for instruction in righteousness.*" The Word of God acts as our anchor to test what we believe the Holy Spirit is telling us, as they will never disagree with one another.

Galatians 4:5-6 – "*5To redeem them that **WERE under the law**, that we might receive the adoption of sons. 6And because ye are sons, God hath sent forth the Spirit of his Son into your hearts, crying Abba, Father*" (KJV, emphasis mine).

Romans 8:14 – "*For as many as are **led by the Spirit of God, they are the sons of God***" (KJV, emphasis mine).

Regarding the Galatians Scripture above, if you have been redeemed from something, common sense, and good English grammar, tells you that that something is bad. No one wants or needs to be redeemed from something that is good or pleasant, do they?

Yet, some people, whom God has redeemed and are saved, will fight to follow what the Spirit of God, through the Apostle Paul, called the ministry of death and the strength of sin: The Mosaic Law. Yes, the Apostle Paul, who wrote most of the New Testament, called the Mosaic Law the strength of sin. Why would any Believer want anything to do with something called "the strength of sin?" We will cover these Scriptures, and others, shortly.

Because I am aware of the gravity of what I am saying, and by virtue of the fact that you may not be convinced by the pictures I have portrayed, let us bring forth several more witnesses in God's Word. In the Old Covenant, YHVH required at least two to three witnesses to validate a point, but since we are sons of the New Covenant let's do better than that: let us bring forth over a dozen.

John 17:17 – *"Sanctify them through thy truth: thy word is truth"* (KJV).

Before we dive into the numerous Scriptures that detail the Mosaic Law being fulfilled, let's deal with a couple of legitimate questions:

1) What about the Scriptures where Jesus Himself references the Mosaic Law as being authoritative?

   and

2) If the Mosaic Law has been fulfilled, how do I know what holiness is?

First, we need to understand that the New Covenant did *not* start with the gospels. The New Covenant did not formally have its inception until Jesus' death and resurrection and was not put into full effect until the outpouring of the Holy Spirit on Pentecost, fifty days later. So, any statement that seems to convey that Jesus is legitimizing the Mosaic Law is because He was speaking to the "lost sheep of the House of Israel" (Matthew 15:24), the Jews, or simply because He had not yet gone to the cross to initiate the beginning of the New Covenant.

A case in point would be the story of the rich young ruler that is mentioned in the synoptic gospels, specifically, Matthew 19:16-21, Mark 10:17-21, and Luke 18:18-21. While some of the details vary, the paraphrase of the story, is that a ruler came to Jesus and asked Him, "What shall I do to inherit eternal life?"

Now, if Jesus was answering from a New Covenant reality, He would have said, "Believe on Me, and your sins will be forgiven, and you will have everlasting life." However, Jesus did not say this. He quoted half of the Ten Commandments to the young ruler, because He was talking to someone under the Mosaic Law, and the Mosaic Law was still in force at the time of their conversation.

Luke 18:20 – *"You know the commandments: 'Don't commit adultery,' 'Don't murder,' 'Don't steal,' 'Don't give false testimony,' 'Honor your father and your mother'"* (WEB).

Remember, the Mosaic Law was still in effect until Jesus died and was resurrected, instituting His New Covenant.

Hebrews 9:16 – *"For where a testament is, there must also of necessity be the death of the testator"* (KJV).

Let's now look at the second question, "If the Mosaic Law has been fulfilled, how do I know what holiness is?"

The answer is: You put your trust in the Father's standard of righteousness for the New Covenant, Jesus, and then follow the leading witness of the Holy Spirit living in you. You can hear, and you will hear, His voice in you—if you listen! The Holy Spirit, incidentally, will never lead you to do anything against the Word of God or the Father, as these three always agree!

1 John 5:7 – *"For there are three that bear record in heaven, the Father, the Word, and the Holy Ghost: and these three are one"* (KJV).

So, please, let us have no silliness of someone saying, "The Holy Spirit told me to divorce my spouse," just because you happen to see someone else you like, or some other unspiritual reason. That would be a, 'different spirit,' not the Holy Spirit! Again, the Holy Spirit will always agree with the Word of God.

Witnesses in The Word

Now, on to further witnesses in the Word that provide evidence that the Mosaic Law is not for a righteous (i.e. saved, born-again) person, whether it be for salvation, or for our walk on this earth.

1 Timothy 1:8-10 – *"⁸But we know that the law is good, if a man use it lawfully; ⁹Knowing this, that the law is not made for a righteous man, but for the lawless and disobedient, for the ungodly and for sinners, for unholy and profane, for murderers of fathers and murderers of mothers, for manslayers, ¹⁰For whoremongers, for them that defile themselves with mankind, for menstealers, for liars, for perjured persons, and if there be any other thing that is contrary to sound doctrine"* (KJV).

Although I have spent much time proving that the Mosaic Law has been done away with for the Believer, is there a group that Paul tells Timothy that the Mosaic Law is for? The Mosaic Law is for the unsaved, the ungodly, those not born again in their spirits who still have the sin nature of Adam. The reason that it is for them is so that they might know God's standard of righteousness, see for themselves that they cannot attain that standard in their own strength, and thus be led to trust Jesus for the free offer of salvation.

The next Scriptures that we will break down and analyze are Colossians 2:13-14, Ephesians 2:14-16, and Exodus 25:21. Follow along closely with these three Scriptures, because once you see the complete picture, you will have more evidence of why the Mosaic Law cannot be a relevant covenant for the Believer.

Let me state again that I am not saying that God winks at sin in the New Covenant. It is just that the way to obtain righteousness and holiness has changed and now both are by grace! It is not that the behavior itself that comes from obeying the Ten Commandments is wrong; far from it. What is wrong with having the Ten Commandments in your life, as a Believer, is the fact that the Ten Commandments are part of the fulfilled

81

Old Covenant Mosaic Law system that demands perfection in order to confer righteousness. When you fall short of what it demands, it brings wrath and condemnation (Galatians 4:15 & Romans 8:1).

In addition, Jesus died to fulfill this covenant (Romans 10:4). Since Romans 8:1 emphatically states that *"there is no condemnation for those who are in Christ Jesus,"* then, by default, the covenant that brings condemnation, cannot be for the Believer who is in Christ.

Instead of being changed from the outside in, as with the Old Covenant Mosaic Law, God now changes us from the inside out, through New Covenant Grace. By realizing you are righteous in Christ, you will live a life that is more holy than by focusing on the Ten Commandments of the Mosaic Law and your efforts to perform them. The world's foremost expositor of grace, and world-famous pastor and teacher, Joseph Prince, has said it best, "Right believing leads to right living." An apple tree does not **try** to bear fruit; it bears fruit because it **is** an apple tree. You must change the inside (your spirit) to change your behavior.

The Mosaic Law – Nailed to the Cross

Colossians 2:13-14 – *"*¹³*And you, being dead in your sins and the uncircumcision of your flesh, hath he quickened together with him, having* **forgiven you all trespasses;** ¹⁴**Blotting out the handwriting of ordinances** *that was* **against us**, *which was* **contrary** *to us, and took it out of the way,* **nailing it to his cross"** (KJV, emphasis mine).

First of all, I think it is of great comfort to know that God has personally forgiven each one of us of all of our trespasses forever. What, however, created these trespasses against God mentioned in verse thirteen above? The answer to this question is revealed in the next verse: Blotting out the handwritten ordinances, or commandments, the Mosaic Law that was against us and contrary to us—meaning contrary to our fallen, Adamic nature.

Was it really the Ten Commandments that were blotted out? In the interest of covering all counter-arguments, I will first address a contention that some pro-Mosaic Law teachers have suggested: that these ordinances mentioned above, in Colossians 2:13-14 and Ephesians 2:15, were not the Ten Commandments, but man-made ordinances created by the Jews to keep Gentiles out of the temple area and keep order there. They contend that it was these man-made rules that were against the Colossian Gentiles.

However, this position cannot be true, as verse thirteen states that the Colossians were "dead in their sins" and that they had been quickened and made alive by the blotting out of the handwritten ordinances. The blotting out of Jewish, man-made, handwritten ordinances would **not** have been able to forgive the Colossians of their trespasses and make them alive.

Paul also stated in verse fourteen that the handwritten ordinances were against "us," including himself. Paul was Jewish, and a former Pharisee, so if the Scripture is referring to Jewish man-made rules that applied to Gentiles they would not have applied to him and he would not have included himself in the group.

Also, remember that in 2 Corinthians 3:7, Paul calls the Ten Commandments the ministration of death written and engraved on stones. The only part of the Mosaic Law that was written, with the finger of God (Ex. 31:18), on stones was the Ten Commandments. Because of this, it is specifically the Ten Commandments, and generally the Mosaic Law, that is being referenced in Colossians when it says they were blotted out.

Then the Scripture states that it (the Ten Commandments as a single collective body of commands) was nailed to the cross. Brothers and sisters, when Jesus blots something out it needs to stay blotted out. When Jesus has taken something out of the way by nailing it to the cross, we need to leave it nailed to the cross! By doing so, Jesus was essentially making the following bold statement:

The old way of trying to be righteous and holy, through your fleshly human efforts, is now over. From now on I will make everyone righteous who comes to me in faith.

It will help clarify things for us if we simply understand that the Old Covenant was all about us: our performance in striving to attain righteousness. The New Covenant is all about Jesus' performance, and simply having mankind put their trust in what He has done! This is why on the cross He uttered the words, "It is finished," as in the future there would no longer be anything for man to do except to believe on Jesus to attain righteous standing before the Father. Remember, at salvation, it is **your spirit** that gets born again.

The Soreg (The Wall of Partition) Is Gone

Ephesians 2:14-16 – *"¹⁴For he is our peace, who hath made both one, and hath broken down the **middle wall of partition between us**; ¹⁵Having abolished in his flesh **the enmity, even the law of commandments** contained in ordinances; for to make in himself of twain **one new man**, so making peace; ¹⁶And that he might reconcile both unto God in one body by the cross, having slain the enmity thereby"* (KJV, emphasis mine).

Here, Paul again confirms the fact that Jesus has fulfilled the Mosaic Law, by stating in Ephesians that Jew and Gentile are now one in Christ. Paul is giving us a great visual picture here, if we take time to see it.

First of all, let's be clear, this Scripture is not talking about a middle wall between God and man, since the verses prior to Ephesians 2:14 refer to Gentile and Jew. But, how have they become one? They are one, because the middle wall of partition, called the *Soreg*, that separated them in the Temple area has been broken down by Jesus fulfilling the Mosaic Law. This is what allows the Jew and Gentile to become one new man in Christ.

Paul further states that the law of commandments contained in ordinances is what created the enmity, the hostility, between the Jew and Gentile. The Jews, because they had the Sinai (marriage) covenant, saw themselves as separate from the rest of the world (all Gentiles) and saw them as unclean, or like dogs. Therefore, the Jews would not have any close association with Gentiles.

This Scripture provides another powerful proof that the Mosaic Law is not for anyone who is in Christ, because Jew and Gentile have now become one. In other words, if the law of commandments, the Mosaic Law, that created the enmity between Jew and Gentile, is still in force, then by definition Jew and Gentile cannot be one new man and Jesus died for nothing! *(See the illustration of the Temple and Soreg on the next page.[3])*

Because the wall of partition was still standing when Paul wrote this Scripture, he is metaphorically stating that Jesus has broken down this middle wall of partition. For most Christians, this is an easy Scripture to gloss over because they are not familiar with the Temple that was standing during Paul's day.

The Soreg was an actual physical wall of separation, erected by the Jews, that stood approximately four and a half feet high and ran along all four sides of the Temple area. It was located inside Solomon's Portico, but outside the Temple wall, and was designed to separate the Jews (the clean) from the Gentiles (the unclean). Paul used this picture of the Soreg, this literal wall of partition that separated Jew and Gentile, to metaphorically explain what Jesus had done by fulfilling the Mosaic Law. Jesus had broken it down and abolished the enmity, the Law of Commandments, thus making Jew and Gentile one!

To understand Paul's picture, we must see the connection he was making. The Soreg physically separated the Jews from the Gentiles in the Temple area, but what separated the Jews from the Gentiles in everyday life? It was their covenant with God, the law of commandments, the Mosaic Law. Ephesians states that Jesus broke down this middle wall of partition by abolishing in His flesh the law of commandments, the Mosaic Law.

---

[3]http://www.biblestudy.org/biblepic/interior-layout-of-temple-large-picture.html provided courtesy of www.biblestudy.org,)

Based on a graphic from
BibleStudy.org

Interior Design of
Jerusalem's Temple

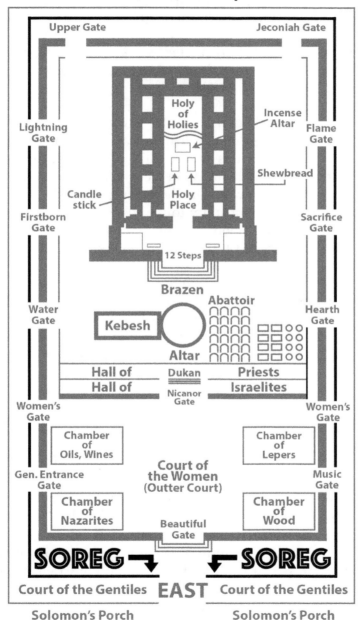

Here is the point: If you believe that any of the Old Covenant Mosaic Law is still in force for the believer—that the Soreg wall of partition is still standing—then Jew and Gentile are *not* one. If Jew and Gentile Believers in Christ are *not* one, then Jesus failed in His mission and we are all still dead in our sins!

Galatians 3:28 – *"There is neither Jew nor Greek, there is neither slave nor free, there is neither male nor female; for you are all one in Christ Jesus"* (NKJV).

By writing this, Paul has put the Jew and the Gentile on the same footing, making them realize they are now one new man in Christ. To most Jews this was initially abhorrent, as they had prided themselves on being God's covenant people for nearly 1500 years. God, however, had bigger plans. He wanted all people to have an opportunity to be His covenant people. It no longer matters what blood (Jew or Gentile) runs through your veins. It is only HIS BLOOD that matters now.

Now, let's step back for a moment and look at this picture of Jew and Gentile being one from a different angle, a Hebrew angle. And further, why the fact that Jew and Gentile being now one new man in Christ Jesus proves that Jesus has done away with the Mosaic Law. When God showed me this next picture, I nearly jumped through the ceiling with excitement!

The Ketubah–The Hebrew Marriage Contract

Why, from a Hebrew perspective, must the Mosaic Law be done away with in order for Jew and Gentile to become one? Because of covenant! God, who has always worked through covenants in His dealings with man, chose the Hebrew people as His special treasure (Exodus 19:5) at Sinai, and at that time implemented the Ten Commandments and the rest of the Mosaic Law covenant. Because of this, for the nation of Israel, according to Ezekiel 16:4-8, the Mosaic Law represented their *Ketubah* (the Hebrew marriage contract) with God.

Ezekiel 16:4-8 – *"⁴As for your birth, in the day you were born your navel was not cut, neither were you washed in water to cleanse you; you weren't salted at all, nor swaddled at all. ⁵No eye pitied you, to do any of these things to you, to have compassion on you; but you were cast out in the open field, for that your person was abhorred, in the day that you were born. ⁶When I passed by you, and saw you wallowing in your blood, I said to you, Though you are in your blood, live; yes, I said to you, Though you are in your blood, live. ⁷I caused you to multiply as that which grows in the field, and you increased and grew great, and you attained to excellent ornament; your breasts were fashioned, and your hair was grown; yet you were naked and bare. ⁸Now when I passed by you, and looked at you, behold, **your time was the time of love**; and I spread my skirt over you, and covered your nakedness: yes, **I swore to you, and entered into a covenant with you, says the Lord Yahweh, and you became mine"*** (WEB, emphasis mine).

This Hebrew marriage contract is the pivotal point for the nation of Israel. As long as their Ketubah, their marriage contract (the Mosaic Law) is in force (or as long as they **believe** it is still in force, the Jews see themselves as married to YHVH.

Let me state that again because of its importance to the overall point. For the Jews, the Mosaic Law is proof to themselves, and to the world, that they are married to God. It is their *Ketubah* Covenant! The Mosaic Law **is** their *Ketubah*! This is the very reason why Paul wrote the following scriptures:

Romans 7:1-4 – *"¹Or don't you know, brothers (for I speak to men **who know the law**), that the law has dominion over a man for as long as he lives? ²For the woman that has a husband is bound by law to the husband while he lives, but if the husband dies, she is discharged from the law of the husband. ³So then if, while the husband lives, she is joined to another man, she would be called an adulteress. **But if the husband dies, she is free from the law**, so that she is no adulteress, though she is joined to another man. ⁴Therefore, my brothers, you also were made dead to the law through the body of Christ, that you would be joined to* *another, to him who was raised from the dead, that we might produce fruit to God"* (WEB, emphasis mine).

Israel's Release from Their *Ketubah*

Paul is obviously addressing the above verses specifically to Jews—men who know the Mosaic Law. How can the Jews become unbound from their marriage contract? Well, since they are living under the Mosaic Law, according to the Torah there is really only one way for their marriage covenant to end and for Israel be released from it.

First, the originator and first party of the Old Covenant marriage contract, God, in the form of Jesus, had to die to fulfill and do away with it. According to Mosaic Law, when one party of a marriage covenant dies, the other is free to remarry. Thus, by Jesus' death, God effectively and legally unbound the Jews from their original marriage covenant that occurred at Sinai (Ezekiel 16:8), so that they were then legally free to be married to another: Jesus.

Romans 7:4 – *"...my brethren, ye also are become dead to the law by the body of Christ; that **ye should be married to another**, even to him who is raised from the dead..."* (KJV, emphasis mine).

Secondly, by His death, Jesus became the mediator of the New Covenant for all men, both Jew and Gentile (since they are now one new man), so that through Him they may become sinless (Hebrews 9:15).

Romans 4:15 – *"...for where no law is, there is no transgression"* (KJV).

Lastly, by this sacrifice God forgave the sin of the entire world.

1 John 2:2 – *"And he is the propitiation for our sins: and not for ours only, but also for the sins of the whole world"* (KJV).

The beautiful picture is that ONLY IN CHRIST can we all become ONE.

Remember the statement of this truth in Ephesians 2:14, which says, *"For he is our peace, who hath made both one, and hath broken down the middle wall of partition…"* This is taken to its ultimate level in the book of Galatians.

Galatians 3:28 – *"There is neither Jew nor Greek, there is neither bond nor free, there is neither male nor female: for ye are all one in Christ Jesus"* (KJV).

The Mosaic Law—The Testimony

We can gain additional insight as to why the Father does not want us to be under the Mosaic Law by going to Exodus 25:21. Here we see that the Ten Commandments, the two tablets of stone that were placed in the Ark of the Covenant, are called the testimony.

Exodus 25:21 – *"And thou shalt put the mercy seat above upon the **ark**; and in the **ark** thou shalt put **the testimony** that I shall give thee"* (KJV, emphasis mine).

Other translations actually render the words as "the two stone tablets," instead of "the testimony." Why were God's Ten Commandments called the *testimony*? God is telling us in Scripture that the Ten Commandments speak. And what do they say? They testify! And what is their testimony? They testify against us! They say, "Mankind, you are falling short of YHVH's righteousness."

That is all that the Mosaic Law can ever do. The Mosaic Law will never tell you, "Hey, way to go—Nice job! You walked in 80 percent godly, righteous perfection today. Don't worry though, you will do better tomorrow!" Does it say that to you? No! The Mosaic Law only points out your shortcomings. At this point in history, this is the Mosaic Law's one and only purpose. The Father gave me this phrase as a reminder of His love and the difference between the Old and New Covenants.

THE MOSAIC LAW
TESTIFIES AGAINST YOU
TO THE FATHER;
JESUS
TESTIFIES FOR YOU
TO THE FATHER!

Now, hold on to your hats, as this "law is fulfilled" picture gets even better! It is of tantamount importance to realize that the Hebrew word for ark, in Exodus 25:21, referring to the Ark of the Covenant, is the Hebrew word *aron*. This is the same Hebrew word used in Genesis 50:26, where the Scripture described bringing Joseph's bones out of Egypt and stated that he was put in a *coffin*.

So, follow this closely: the word coffin here is the Hebrew word *aron*, which is the same one used for the Ark of the Covenant. What is the significance of these two pictures? Well, the purpose of a coffin is to bury something, usually a dead body. So, what is God telling us?

Let's get the full picture of what He is saying by remembering that there were three items that God instructed Moses to put into the Ark of the Covenant: Aaron's rod that budded, the jar of manna from the wilderness, and the stone tablets on which the Ten Commandments were written. All of these things represented man's rebellion to God.

Aaron's rod represented man's rebellion toward God's appointed priestly authority and leadership. The jar of manna represented man's rebellion toward God's provision. Finally, the two stone tablets represented man's rebellion toward God's way to live, His moral law.

What was placed on **top** of the Ark of the Covenant? It was the mercy seat with the two cherubim facing each other. God had Moses put everything that represented man's rebellion (his sins) and had him ostensibly bury them under the Ark's (the coffin's) mercy seat. Wow! In picture form, God's wants everything regarding man's sin buried and under His mercy seat where the blood was sprinkled! This is the same picture of what Jesus did for us. All of our sins are now under His blood.

But that is not all. Do you remember when I quoted 1 John 2:2, *"And he is the propitiation for our sins: and not for ours only, but also for the sins of the whole world"?* The word propitiation is the Greek word, *hilasmos*. In Romans 3:25, the same word is written *hilasterion*.

The definition of *hilasterion* is MERCY SEAT! So, if we substitute those words, 1 John 2:2 would read, *"And he* [Jesus] *is the mercy seat* [where the blood was placed in the Old Covenant] *for our sins; and not for ours only, but also for the sins of the whole world."*

In the Old Covenant, once per year, God would look down from Heaven on the Feast of Atonement and see the blood of the perfect lamb on the Ark's Mercy Seat. Because of the blood, He would not **see** Israel's sin (everything that was buried under the Mercy Seat), and their sin would be covered for another year.

Now, in the New Covenant, He looks at our Mercy Seat, Jesus, and His one-time, effective forever sacrifice, and His blood, and He never sees our sin again. What an unbelievable picture that is a perfect match for what happened in the Old Covenant. Jesus is our New Covenant Mercy Seat and has forgiven the sin of the whole world once and for all!

Hebrews 9:26 – *"…but now once in the end of the world hath he appeared to put away sin by the sacrifice of himself"* (KJV).

It only remains for anyone in the world to humble themselves and accept this forgiveness.

LISTEN, ALL WHO HAVE EARS TO HEAR!
Yes, especially those of you who have not yet accepted Jesus as your Messiah!

GOD IS NOT MAD AT YOU!!!

God is wanting, and waiting, to adopt you as His son or daughter into His family. But His Word, and His Word made flesh, His Son, has said that the only way is through Jesus. Most of the world accuses Christianity of being narrow in its view of the age-old question, "How do I get to Heaven?" They think that it is terribly bigoted that Christians say that Jesus is the only way.

Instead of saying that Christians have a narrow view, I would tell the world that it is not so much narrow as it is simple. It is what Paul called, "...*the simplicity that is in Christ*" (2 Corinthians 11:3). God is essentially saying, "Simply believe on My Son, and you will be saved." All other false belief systems in this world are far more complicated in their purported way of getting to Heaven.

They all make their own roads to God, the Father, and they are all through works. They believe that all roads lead to Rome. They say, "Just be a good person, and when you die it will be alright." What all other religions and belief systems fail to realize is that all of them are based on human effort and works, and none of them can change the sin nature of man received from Adam— most of them even deny it.

True Christianity is unique in all the world. Let me say that again: True Christianity is unique in all the world because it is the only belief system where your salvation is free.

Here is the ironic point: God has to give us salvation. Does that surprise you? It is because of His Word and His free gift of salvation that He is a debtor to no man. If God required something from you for you to get to Heaven, He would be a debtor to you as He would be giving you something that you earned. But God is a debtor to no man (Romans 11:35). Will you let Him adopt you by simply accepting Jesus' blood sacrifice for your sins?

John 14:6 – *"...I am the way, the truth, and the life: no man cometh unto the Father, but by me"* (KJV).

The New Testament truth of the Old Covenant picture of the mercy seat, and fulfilled picture, about the mercy seat is that Jesus and His blood is now covering all things that represent man's rebellion. His blood covers my rebellion, your rebellion, and any sins—past, present or future. Jesus has placed His blood on the true Mercy Seat that is in Heaven, (Hebrews 9:11-12). The reason that this is an important truth is because now, when the Father looks at a Believer, He only sees them through the blood of Jesus that covers them, that is on the Mercy Seat in Heaven. Their spirit has been purified by His blood, and now it is in union with God.

Even more amazing is the picture of New Covenant truth in the picture of the Old Covenant Ark. Remember, the Ark of the Covenant had two angels on each end of the Mercy Seat, and the blood of the atonement was poured in the middle. This picture is faithfully recreated at Jesus' tomb in the Gospel of John.

John 20:11-12 – *"11But Mary stood without at the sepulcher weeping: and as she wept, she stooped down, and looked into the sepulcher, 12And **seeth two angels in white sitting, the one at the head, and the other at the feet, where the body of Jesus had lain**"* (KJV, emphasis mine).

Do you see it? John the Apostle has just described the picture of the Old Covenant mercy seat. The stone slab where Jesus had been lying had two angels, one at the head and another at the feet, and His bloody body had been in the middle! Here is yet another New Covenant composite picture of an Old Covenant type.

As they say, "If that picture does not light your fire, your wood may be wet." However, I believe the Father delights in hiding gems for His kings and priests (1 Peter 2:9) to find in Scripture. So, while we are in the Gospel of John let me reveal a couple more composite pictures that show the Father's love for us.

John 20:2-4 – *"2Then she runneth, and cometh to Simon Peter, and to the other disciple, whom Jesus loved, and saith unto them, They have taken away the Lord out of the sepulchre, and we know* *not where they have laid him.* ³*Peter therefore went forth, and that other disciple, and came to the sepulchre.* ⁴*So they ran both together: and the other disciple did outrun Peter, and came first to the sepulchre"* (KJV).

First of all, it is commonly known that the disciple whom Jesus loved was John. (It is not that Jesus did not love the other disciples, but that John had a revelation of Jesus' love for him.) The key to seeing the hidden picture behind the Scripture is understanding the meaning of the Hebrew names of Peter and John. John's name in Hebrew is *Yochanan* and means grace. Peter's name in Aramaic/Hebrew is *Kepha,* and means stone, representative of the Mosaic Law. In the Scripture above God is saying, "Grace will always outrun and surpass the law!" It is picture of the Mosaic Law being completely fulfilled by Jesus and His covenant of grace.

Secondly, Jesus' personal promise that He will return is hidden in plain sight a few verses later.

John 20:6-7 – *"*⁶*Simon Peter therefore comes, following him, and entered into the tomb, and sees the linen cloths lying,* ⁷*and the **handkerchief** which was upon his head, not lying with the linen cloths, **but folded up in a distinct place by itself"*** (DBY, emphasis mine).

In other Bible translations, the word handkerchief is translated "napkin." In ancient Hebrew culture, when someone was dining and had fully eaten and was finished, they would wad up their napkin and place it on the table. However, if they folded their napkin/handkerchief and placed it where they were reclining as they excused themselves, it meant that they would be returning! The Apostle John goes out of his way to tell us, in this seemingly unimportant detail, that Jesus' napkin was folded up and in a distinct place by itself. Jesus is telling all who read the Scriptures that He will be returning! Halleluyah! Maranatha! (The Lord is coming!)

Do you remember what else happened when Jesus died? There was an earthquake, and the veil of the temple was **torn**

95

from top to bottom. Now, this veil was a heavy curtain made of woven material four inches thick and standing approximately sixty feet high. It is what separated the Holy Place from the Holy of Holies, where the Ark of the Covenant was kept (representing YHVH and where His presence dwelt).

This was a supernatural event orchestrated by the Father! Not only was the Earth (Jesus' creation) groaning at His death, but also any other object would have, most likely, been torn from the point of the Earth's disruption: from bottom to top. The Scripture writer goes out of his way to say that it was torn top to bottom, as though God was tearing it Himself.

In this picture of the events, God is saying, "This Old Covenant is over, and My Presence is freed from this one place; now I will live in all Believers, and they will be known as the Body of Christ."

The Jewish priests and Levites, in religious fashion, later repaired the veil to try and perpetuate the Old Covenant system. But approximately forty years later, in 70 A.D., the Roman General, Titus, destroyed the temple entirely, halting the Old Covenant animal sacrifice system of works-based righteousness. The Father, by removing the very place where Old Covenant sacrifices and Atonement were made, is blatantly saying that the Mosaic Law system is over. Atonement has been made. Since the blood of God's Son has been poured out, there is no need for any blood of animals, and by extension, no need for any works on the part of man.

Up until now, we have been recounting how Jesus fulfilled the New Covenant Passover and Pentecost. However, if you will allow me to digress for a moment, I believe you will find it interesting to see a picture of how Jesus fulfilled another Hebrew Feast as well.

During His questioning by Pilate, Jesus also fulfilled the Hebrew Feast of Yom Kippur. Yom Kippur (see Leviticus 16 and 23:27) was the Feast of Atonement, where Israel's sins were covered (not forgiven) each year. Part of the requirements for this feast was that two goats, as similar as possible, were chosen. Then, by casting lots, one was chosen as the sin offering and the other was taken to be the scapegoat offering (remember both of these for later). The scapegoat was the offering which carried Israel's sins away into the wilderness.

In the following passage, we see Pontius Pilate trying to release Jesus by giving the crowd the choice between Him and a known murderer and insurrectionist, named Barabbas.

Luke 23:18-25 – *"18And they cried out all at once, saying, Away with this man, and release unto us Barabbas: 19(Who for a certain sedition made in the city, and for murder, was cast into prison.) 20Pilate therefore, willing to release Jesus, spake again to them. 21But they cried, saying, Crucify him, crucify him. 22And he said unto them the third time, Why, what evil hath he done? I have found no cause of death in him: I will therefore chastise him, and let him go. 23And they were instant with loud voices, requiring that he might be crucified. And the voices of them and of the chief priests prevailed. 24And Pilate gave sentence that it should be as they required. 25And he released unto them him that for sedition and murder was cast into prison, whom they desired; but he delivered Jesus to their will"* (KJV).

All of the verses you have just read may, initially, seem rather straightforward and innocuous. Jesus, the **Son of God**, had just been turned over to those who wanted His life. However, being familiar with the Old Covenant and the Feast of Atonement, and knowing that Jesus was our sin offering, we can see the picture that Jesus is the sin offering, and Barabbas is the scapegoat offering.

But if that is so, how on earth do these two radically different people fulfill the need in the Old Covenant composite picture where both potential sacrifices had to be similar? One is the Holy Lamb of God and the other is a murderer and insurrectionist—not similar at all.

However, the picture becomes much clearer when we understand what the meaning of Barabbas' name. In Hebrew, his name is in two parts. The first is *Bar*, which means "son." The second is *abba*(s), which means "father(s)." Barabbas means "THE FATHER'S SON!" Now you see it, don't you?

Now we have an exact match in the names of the two people in this story: Jesus, the Father's Son as the sin offering and Barabbas, the Father's Son (though in name only) is the Yom Kippur scapegoat offering that went free! The Father draws wonderful pictures, doesn't He?

Chapter Five
The Other Witnesses

Jesus is the End of the Mosaic Law

Now let us look at the other witnesses in Scripture that confirm that the Mosaic Law is not for the Believer. Of all of the Scriptures none could be more succinct than this:

Romans 10:4 – *"For Christ is the end of the law for righteousness to everyone that believeth"* (KJV).

But the list of witnesses goes on:

Romans 3:20 – *"Therefore by deeds of the law there shall no flesh be justified in his sight: for by the law is knowledge of sin"* (KJV).

Romans 3:21 – *"But now **the righteousness of God without the law** is manifested, being witnessed by the law and the prophets"* (KJV, emphasis mine).

Athough Romans 3:21 is fulfilled by the mere fact that the Mosaic Law and Prophets of the Old Testament prophesied about Jesus, we could also say that this Scripture was also fulfilled in a single New Covenant event that was witnessed by three of the Apostles.

However, there is another fulfillment of this Scripture if we refer back to Matthew 17 and the account of the transfiguration. The picture is easily seen once you know to look for it. Here we see Jesus' appearance changing and His face becoming like the sun. On this high mountain, Moses (who represents the Mosaic Law) and Elijah (who represents the prophets) also appeared and talked with Him. Both Moses and Elijah in this story are witnesses to how the Father would make man righteous without the Mosaic Law: Jesus Himself.

They not only witnessed Jesus' appearance, but in Luke's account of this story it states that Moses and Elijah spoke of His death. In other words, they spoke about *how* He was going to accomplish *righteousness without the law.*

Jesus is Part of the Triune God

Aside from the prophecies about Jesus, He can be seen in the Torah as early as Genesis 1:26, *"And God said, Let **us** make man in our image, after our likeness"* (emphasis mine).

If you look closely at this Scripture, it reveals the triune nature of God. Not necessarily because God said, "us," although it **is** a plural pronoun, because that designation could, technically, mean just two.

We know God is triune because God said we are created in **His image and His likeness. Because we are triune (spirit, soul and body) in nature, we can then backtrack and know that He is also triune: Father, Son and Holy Spirit.**

For those who have difficulty understanding this tri-unity concept, simply go to your refrigerator, pick out an egg, and crack it into a bowl. It is one egg, yet has three parts: shell, white and yolk. Sometimes, I believe we need to stop trying to figure God out and instead just take Him at His Word. You would do that for your best friend, wouldn't you? Well, God loves you more than your best friend, and He is trustworthy!

If you are thinking to yourself that Jesus is **not** directly mentioned or revealed in Genesis 1:26, you would be correct. However, we definitely see that God refers to Himself as **"us,"** and in John 10:30, Jesus affirms that He and the Father are one.

Pictures of Jesus in Old Testament Scripture

Jesus, who is grace and truth (John 1:17) is always there when a grace covenant is made. Scripture says that Noah found grace in the sight of the Lord, so we could say that he was the first participant in a grace covenant.

Genesis 8:6 – *"But Noah found grace in the eyes of the LORD."*

The Ark that Noah built is a composite picture of Jesus in that *"all of the righteous on earth"* (Noah's family) went inside the Ark before judgment came, and they were saved. In the same way, there will be no judgment on Believers who are in Christ when He returns. Jesus is our New Covenant Ark.

To see another picture of Jesus directly drawn in Old Covenant Scripture, let us turn to Genesis 15 and look at the story of how Abram, whose name means "exalted father," came to be in covenant with God. (I will use Abram's God-given name, Abraham, going forward.)

First of all, before we find the picture of Jesus, let us understand that Abraham can be seen as a picture of all New Covenant Believers in several ways. How is that possible? Well, remember that Jesus' covenant, at its root, has two components: we are saved by grace through faith (Ephesians 2:8). Believers utilize their faith—given to them by God (Romans 12:3)—and accept God's grace gift (Jesus) that He provided for the remission of sins, for salvation. Abraham, too, was a man of faith.

Genesis 15:6 – *"And he **believed** in the LORD; and he counted it to him for righteousness"* (KJV, emphasis mine).

Abraham also received God's grace (His unmerited favor) because He personally chose him and set him apart to begin a holy (set apart) nation. He called him and brought him out of the world system where he was living, in Ur of the Chaldees. In the same way, God has personally chosen all Believers, and set us apart as holy (Genesis 11:31, John 15:16, 1 Peter 1:16). Believers are in the world, but not of the world, and are a holy nation (John 17:16, 1 Peter 2:9).

Abraham also received grace by the change of his name. If you will recall, the fifth letter of the Hebrew aleph-bet is the letter *hey* or *hei*. It is written in English as "H," and its Hebrew meaning is "grace." God changed Abram's name, and his wife Sarai's, by adding the letter *hey* (H) to it. God literally added grace to Abraham's name!

In doing so, He also changed his name's meaning, from "exalted father," to "father of many nations," as God had prophesied that he would be in Genesis 17:4. Within a year of their name changes, Abra(h)am and Sara(h) were able to bring forth God's promised child, Isaac, after trying unsuccessfully themselves for 25 years. New Covenant Believers need to see that God's promises in the New Covenant are also accessed by God's grace and our faith. As Believers, we are no longer servants, we are joint heirs with Jesus (Romans 8:17).

Based on the above explanation, hopefully you can see that Abraham is a picture of someone who has received God's grace, and therefore a composite picture of all Believers who have also received God's grace. However, if you are a stickler for detail, you may argue that my picture is not accurate, as New Covenant Believers actually have a direct encounter with Jesus in some way. So far, in my example, Abraham (although he had received grace from the Father) had not had a direct encounter with Jesus—or so it would seem. To prove that he did, let us go back to the day when the LORD made covenant with Abraham.

You are probably familiar with God telling Abraham to take sacrificial animals and to cut them in two. Subsequently, a deep sleep fell upon Abraham and then an amazing thing happened that I will let Scripture describe:

Genesis 15:17-18 – *"17And it came to pass, that, when the sun went down, and it was dark, behold **a smoking furnace,** and **a burning lamp** that **passed between those pieces.** 18In the same day **the** LORD **made a covenant with Abram,** saying, Unto thy seed have I given this land, from the river of Egypt unto the great river, the river Euphrates"* (KJV, emphasis mine).

So, we see that while Abraham was asleep, God made covenant with him. Abraham's state of being asleep will be significant later. The two personages that are interacting with Abraham, in the above Scripture, are described by the writer as a smoking furnace and a burning lamp. It has long been postulated by Biblical teachers that these two entities represent the Father and the Son. This assumption makes sense and it sounds nice; however, we need to ask if we can find proof of this in Scripture.

It is also important for Believers to see that this entire scene in the book of Genesis is also a composite picture of the Believer's covenant with the Father, through Jesus. Why is this important? The benefit is that, if we can see this, it will strengthen our faith!

Most Believers see Abraham as this paragon of faith, the "friend of God." We are in awe of him, and rightly so. Knowing this, if we Believers can see ourselves in our New Covenant, as types of Abraham in this story, with all the similarities that I have mentioned, it will give us tremendous confidence in our own position with the Father in the New Covenant of Grace that we are resting in. You are resting, right?

The Mediator

As you look at the verses in Genesis 15 closely, you will understand that it is God who is instigating and executing the making of the covenant with Abraham. Abraham, himself, is a passive participant, as he is asleep during the covenant making.

And as we will see later, it is Jesus who stood in for Abraham, just as it was Jesus who stood in for us, at Golgotha. It had to be this way because neither we, nor Abraham, could enter into covenant face-to-face with God and live. Abraham, in essence, needed someone to stand in for him. Abraham needed a mediator. Does this term sound familiar?

1 Timothy 2:5 – *"For there is one God, and **one mediator** between God and men, the man Christ Jesus"* (KJV, emphasis mine).

So, the picture we are seeing is this: Abraham, the man of faith, believed God and received God's grace, and then, while he was asleep (note: before the Mosaic Law was given), God made covenant with him through the agency of Jesus, his mediator. We see a mirror of this grace covenant in God's covenant with Believers. We, like Abraham, are people who exercise our faith, and believe God to receive the grace He has provided. Then while we are asleep (dead in our sins), we enter into covenant with God through the agency of Jesus, our mediator.

The New Covenant appropriately took place after the Mosaic Law was fulfilled. Just as there was no Law when Abraham's grace covenant was inaugurated, the New Covenant appropriately *began* after the Mosaic Law had *ended*. So, we can see in both cases that the grace covenants have no connection to the Mosaic Law. It was not in existence when either grace covenant was made. In Abraham's case, it was before the Mosaic Law; in the Believer's case, it is after the Mosaic Law had been fulfilled. The grace covenants have the same composite picture in each case, with the same consequences: *justification by faith alone!*

Smoking Furnace and Burning Lamp

Now, let us move on to the Scriptural proof that the smoking furnace and the burning lamp in Genesis 15 are, in fact, the Father and the Son. To do this, we will turn to the book of Exodus to the chapter prior to when the nation of Israel received the Ten Commandments.

Exodus 19:18 – *"And Mount Sinai was altogether on a smoke, because the* LORD *descended upon it in fire: and the smoke thereof ascended as **the smoke of a furnace**, and the whole mount quaked greatly"* (KJV, emphasis mine).

Here, Scripture plainly states that God the Father was on Mount Sinai and He is represented as the smoke of a furnace. The Scriptural confirmation is there verbatim, in black and white. Here is the Father, the first party of the covenant with Abraham, being reaffirmed with the same name that He is portrayed with in Genesis 15:17: *the smoke of a furnace.*

To find Jesus personified as the lamp that burns, we have to search a little bit harder and, once again, having a cursory knowledge of Hebrew does come in handy. As I stated earlier, the name Yeshua can have different meanings as there are several different spellings for the name, (Yeshoshua, Yeshua, Yeshuah) and in the Hebrew language this is not at all unusual.

The first and most powerful meaning is "Yahweh saves," but when used in a generic sense, or translated as a common noun, it can also simply mean salvation.

Isaiah 62:1 – *"For Zion's sake I will not hold My peace, And for Jerusalem's sake I will not rest, Until her righteousness goes forth as brightness, And her **salvation** as a **lamp that burns**"* (NKJV, emphasis mine).

In this verse, the word salvation, in the Strong's Concordance, is *yeshuah*! So, the Scripture above reads, *"and her **yeshuah** like a lamp that burns."* Halleluyah! This is exactly what God, through the writer of Genesis 15:17, calls the second party of the Abrahamic covenant: a lamp that burns. Indeed, Jesus Himself declared He was the light of the world—the lamp that burns.

Friends, when you see the pictures of Scripture explained in this kind of detail, but yet with such simplicity, you absolutely have to try not to understand what the Bible is saying: Jesus is Lord of all!

We can now go back to Genesis 15:17 and understand that Jesus is specifically seen in the Old Covenant, and Abraham did have a direct personal encounter with Him. In fact, there is a not-so-veiled reference to this direct encounter mentioned in John 8:56, when Jesus is asserting to the Jews His supremacy over their father, Abraham.

John 8:56 – *"Your father Abraham rejoiced to see My day: and he saw it, and was glad"* (NKJV).

This Scripture perfectly describes Abraham's encounter with Jesus on the day that God made covenant with him. Who can know all that Jesus showed Abraham while he was asleep on that most intimate of days when covenant was made? What we can know, from the Scripture, is that Abraham saw Jesus' day and was glad. I personally believe that when Scripture says, *"he saw* [my day],*"* that it is saying that Abraham saw ALL that Jesus was and ALL that He would accomplish for the world. That is why Abraham was glad!

Genesis 22:18 – *"In your seed all the nations of the earth shall be blessed, because you have obeyed My voice"* (NKJV).

The seed was Jesus, as He was a descendant of Abraham (Matthew 1:1-16).

Galatians 3:7 – *"Know therefore that those who are of faith, the same are children of Abraham"* (WEB).

Those who are of faith are children of Abraham. Notice, it does not say those of faith and works. We are not to mix the covenants.

If you will meditate on the picture detailed above, and see the similarities in the two grace covenants, I believe you will be greatly encouraged, and your faith will be strengthened. All Believers need to see and take stock of the fact that, in Christ, you too are a friend of God, as Abraham was. Since Abraham lived before Jesus, and His dealing with the sin of the whole world, you as a Believer actually occupy a more favored position that Abraham ever could. Abraham accessed the promises of God by believing in, and looking forward to, the cross. We access them by looking back to the cross as an accomplished event, because all our sins have been forgiven forever.

We have also seen that Jesus is present at the second grace covenant with Abraham, as we discovered in Isaiah 62:1 that states that Yeshua is the lamp that burns. Jesus, the lamp that burns and as Abraham's mediator, stands in for him and makes covenant with the Father (the smoking oven) while Abraham is asleep (dead in his sins). Finally, at the inauguration of the New Covenant of Grace, we see Jesus fully manifested in the flesh on Calvary, making covenant with the Father on **our** behalf.

What About Sinai?

Interestingly, you can look through the Bible from cover to cover, but you will **not** see Jesus, or any composite pictures of God's Son, in any of the Scriptures that reference the inauguration of the Mosaic Law. His absence is extremely telling! Yes, I understand that God gave the Mosaic Law to Israel and that Jesus is God, and so in that sense Jesus was there, but remember we are looking for pictures.

Jesus is not visible as a composite picture at the giving of the Mosaic Law. Yes, He did die as God's representative of Himself (as I stated earlier, as first party of the Sinai Covenant), and I am aware of the multitude of pictures of Jesus in the Old Testament, like the Ark and others. However, my point is this: if we see Him **at the inauguration** of the other grace covenants, we would certainly look for Him in a similar composite picture at the onset of the Covenant of the Mosaic Law made at Sinai.

The reason why we do not is because the Mosaic Law covenant is one of *demand*, and all of the grace covenants are ones of *supply*. Jesus is mediator over the covenant that supplies obedience—His perfect obedience—and He has made us sufficient as ministers of the New Covenant, not of the Old (2 Corinthians 3:6).

This is a huge point that cannot be over emphasized. Every Scripture, referenced below, about the giving of the Mosaic Law states that it was given through **angels**. Jesus is nowhere to be found in any of the text or represented in picture form in any way.

Deuteronomy 33:2 – *"He said, "Yahweh came from Sinai, and rose from Seir to them. He shone from Mount Paran. He came from **the ten thousands of holy ones**. At his right hand was **a fiery law** for them"* (WEB, emphasis mine).

Acts 7:38 – *"This is he who was in the assembly in the wilderness with **the angel** that spoke to him on **Mount Sinai**, and with our fathers, who received living revelations to give to us"* (WEB, emphasis mine).

Acts 7:53 – *"You received the law as it was **ordained by angels**, and didn't keep it!"* (WEB, emphasis mine).

Galatians 3:19 – *"What then is the law? It was added because of transgressions, **until the offspring** [the seed] should come to whom the promise has been made. It was **ordained through angels** by the hand of a mediator[4]"* (WEB, brackets mine, emphasis mine).

Freedom Under Grace

Let us move on now to other Scriptures, our other witnesses, proving that the Mosaic Law has been fulfilled for the Believer!

Romans 4:14-15 – *"For if they which are of the law be heirs, faith is made void, and the promise made of none effect: Because the*

---

[4] Some students of the Bible may question who the mediator is in this last Scripture. In all the commentaries on Galatians 3:19, the mediator is always described as Moses, not Jesus.

law worketh wrath: for where no law is, there is no transgression"
(KJV).

For those who still want part of the Mosaic Law in the New
Covenant, they must realize that it brings wrath. When you are
living in relationship with your Father, through Jesus, there is no
wrath. Your Father is never wrathful toward you. 1 Thessalonians
5:9 clearly says that God has not appointed us to wrath. Although
He disciplines those He loves, it is not through sickness or
accidents, it is through His Word (Isaiah 53:4-5, 2 Timothy 3:16).
Your sins—past, present, and future—have already been judged,
because the sins of the entire world were placed on Jesus when
He hung on the cross at Golgotha/Calvary.

1 John 2:2 – *"And he is the propitiation for our sins: and not for our only,
but also for the sins of the whole world."*

John 3:18 – *"He that believes on him is not judged: but he that believes
not has been already judged, because he has not believed on the name of the
only-begotten Son of God."*

Romans 5:20 – *"Moreover the law entered, that the offence might
abound. But where sin abounded, grace did much more abound."*

Romans 6:14 – *"For sin shall not have dominion over you: for ye are not
under law, but under grace."*

For Romans 6:14 to be true, then the opposite of this
Scripture would also have to be true. In other words, *if you are under
law, then sin will have dominion over you!*

Do you believe that being under the Mosaic Law, and
consequently dominated by sin, is the position in which Jesus
wants His brothers (Hebrews 2:11) after He has given His life for
them to be free? No, my friend, under the covenant of grace you,
through Jesus, have dominion over sin.

Romans 7:4-6 – *"⁴Wherefore, my brethren, **ye also are become
dead to the law by the body of Christ**; that ye should be*

*married to another, even **to him who is raised from the dead,** that we should bring forth fruit unto God. ⁵For **when we were in the flesh,** the motions of sins, which were by the law, did work in our members to **bring forth fruit unto death.** ⁶But now **we are delivered from the law,** that being dead wherein we were held; that **we should serve in newness of spirit,** and **not in the oldness of the letter"** (KJV, emphasis mine).

Romans 3:19 – *"¹⁹Now we know that what things soever the law saith, it saith to them who are under the law: that every mouth may be stopped, and all the world may become guilty before God."*

Look closely at the above Scriptures. Paul is using severe language in describing how the Believer should behave in relation to the Mosaic Law. They should be dead to it! So, if you understand the Scripture correctly, as a born again believer it doesn't matter what the Mosaic Law says, because it is not saying anything to a Believer! We as Believers should be as though we cannot hear it, because we are dead to it. According to the Scriptures you have just read, if you are born again, you are no longer married to Mr. Mosaic Law, but now are married to another—to Him who is raised from the dead, Mr. Jesus Grace!

Paul then, in verses five and six, contrasts the two covenants by calling one **flesh** and the other **spirit**. He says that when we were in the flesh, the motions of sins were **by the Mosaic Law**. Being in the flesh means to be merely naturally born of Adam and following the Mosaic Law prior to being born again. So, in the flesh, sin worked in our members, and the type of fruit it brought forth was death.

However, because Believers are not in the flesh, but born of the Spirit, we serve not according to the letter (the Mosaic Law and our flesh), but in newness of spirit, which is Jesus' Holy Spirit in union with our spirits.

You are not in the flesh if indeed the Spirit of God dwells in you (Romans 8:9).

Romans 7:9-10 – *"⁹For I was alive without the law once: but when the commandment came, sin revived, and I died. ¹⁰And the commandment, which was ordained to life, I found to be unto death"* (KJV).

Romans 8:1 – *"There is therefore now no condemnation to them which are in Christ Jesus, who walk not after the flesh, but after the Spirit"* (KJV).

The Old Covenant, and the Ten Commandments that are contained within it, is based upon our performance and always brings guilt and condemnation, because we will always fall short in our efforts to perform it. We will always fail in the eyes of the Mosaic Law. What many Believers do is go back and try to serve the Ten Commandments that have been fulfilled. Because of wrong teaching and tradition, they feel compelled to go back and serve the Mosaic Law. They subsequently fail, and then they feel condemned, so they then come back to Jesus for forgiveness and are strengthened by His love and grace, then they go back again to serve the Mosaic Law, and are condemned again, and the cycle continues.

They need to realize who the Scripture says they are married to and stop going back to their Old Husband, the Mosaic Law of the Old Covenant. In fact, if you laid each of these covenants, and their terms, side-by-side and observed their differences, you would see visually that the Mosaic Law cannot coincide with Jesus' covenant for the Believer. It is an impossibility to abide by both at the same time.

In the covenant that Jesus instituted, there is no condemnation, because we are in Him, and He has fulfilled the Mosaic Law. You might be asking, "How can there be no condemnation from God, or in me, when I know I sin?" First of all, this no condemnation verbiage can be confusing to the natural mind because we are taught—conditioned by the world we live in, and often by our parents when we were growing up—to feel guilt and condemnation when we miss the mark, when we sin.

Paul explains this struggle, and resolution, in the book of Romans. What Paul reveals, in Romans 7:15-25 and 8:1, is that he knows, because he is born again, that in his mind he desires to do good, but yet he falls short and sins in his flesh. He sees the dichotomy of the two opposing forces: his flesh verses his spirit and the war that they wage against one another. He resolves this conflict by asking and answering his own question.

Romans 7:24-25 – *"24…who shall deliver me out of this body of death? 25I thank God, through Jesus Christ our Lord…"*

Paul realized that, try as he might, his flesh would sin. This is not to say we casually give in to it and live a sinful lifestyle. However, Paul purposed to live his life out of his spirit, in union with Jesus, and not walk in condemnation over sin in the flesh.

Romans 8:1-3 – *"1There is therefore now no condemnation to them which are in Christ Jesus, who walk not after the flesh, but after the Spirit. 2For the law of the Spirit of life in Christ Jesus hath made me free from the law of sin and death. 3For what the law could not do, in that it was weak through the flesh, God sending his own Son in the likeness of sinful flesh, and for sin, condemned sin in the flesh"* (KJV).

Read that last verse, again. Because you have accepted Jesus' blood sacrifice, your *"sin in the* flesh" has already condemned/judged. At the same time, your spirit was united with His and was made perfect (1 Corinthians 6:17). The only battle that remains is for you to renew your soul (mind, will and emotions) to the Word of God (Romans 12:2) and bring your thoughts into line with the Bible's truth.

What Paul understood, and conveys here, is that when you understand the New Covenant and who you are in Christ, (assuming that you have given your heart to Him and your desire is to follow Him) there is no condemnation from God (and should be none from yourself) when you sin. You are in Christ Jesus. Yes, you are to have conviction from the Holy Spirit and remorse from your heart, but not condemnation.

112

What I have written could be twisted by those who are trying to misunderstand what I am saying, so let me add this statement: No, I am not saying that our behavior does not matter! What I am saying is simply what Paul has already stated from Holy Scripture in Romans 8:1. This same thought is repeated in a couple of different versions of Hebrews 10:2, when the writer, contrasting the sacrifices of the Old Covenant to the single sacrifice of Jesus in the New, makes the following claim:

Hebrews 10:2 – *"Or else wouldn't they* **[the Mosaic Law sacrifices]** *have ceased to be offered, because the worshippers, having been* **once cleansed, would have had no more consciousness of sins?"** (WEB, brackets mine, emphasis mine).

The Interlinear Translation of this scripture actually renders it more powerfully, *"none having any longer conscience of sins"*. The writer of Hebrews is laying out the following amazing comparison between the two covenants. If the Mosaic Law sacrifices had been effective, the people of the Old Covenant would not have had any more *consciousness* of their sins. They would have no sins on their *conscience*—ever!

On the other hand, since Jesus' one-time sacrifice was effective, we should not only have no condemnation, we should have no more consciousness, or conscience, of sins. Believers in Jesus should have no sins dwelling on their conscience, since they know that Jesus has paid for them all.

This no condemnation, and no sin consciousness, revelation of God's Word could possibly do away with the reason half of the people on Earth are sick in their bodies, if those who were sick would meditate on it and understand it. Many people are carrying enormous weights with them. They are carrying guilt and condemnation from the thought that they have failed God in trying to obey the Mosaic Law, from having failed on a vow made, or failed a parent, spouse, or themselves. Because of this, they are sick in their bodies. They are in need of accepting the forgiveness for all things that only Jesus can supply.

Please understand, in saying that there is no condemnation for Believers, I am not saying that someone who believes these Scriptures regarding no condemnation and no consciousness of sin, is some type of sociopath that literally has no conscience. On the contrary, when a Believer sins they feel extreme remorse, because they know they not only have offended a person, but also God.

However, in the New Covenant you can feel remorse—you can feel sorry for something you have done, or some offense that you have caused—without condemnation, knowing that you are in Christ and He has forgiven you of all your sins. The sins are committed in the flesh, but they do not contaminate your spirit. This was Paul's point in when he said, *"For I don't know what I am doing. For I don't practice what I desire to do; but what I hate, that I do"* (Romans 7:15). Yet a few verses later, in Romans 8:1, he emphatically states that there is no condemnation for those who are in Christ Jesus. Paul sinned and felt remorse, yet he was not condemned by it because he had a revelation of what Jesus had done for him.

It is also possible to believe that the Father has forgiven us, yet if we do not forgive ourselves, we will remain in a prison of our own making. If we are to grow into all that the Father has for us, we must not only accept God's forgiveness, but also forgive ourselves. If the Greater One, the Father in Heaven who created you, has forgiven you, who are you to not forgive others and yourself?

If this is you, please understand, you do not have to pay anymore. You do not have to punish yourself anymore. The debt for all things on this earth has been paid in full, and you only need to accept it. This is truly good news!

Free from the Mosaic Law

Matthew 9:17 – *"Nor do men put new wine into old skins, otherwise the skins burst and the wine is poured out, and the skins will be destroyed; but they put new wine into new skins, and both are preserved together"* (DBY).

Here Jesus uses a picture of wineskins to describe a person, and old and new wine to describe the covenants. Jesus is prophetically saying to not mix the covenants together as they do not work together, and if you do mix them, you will end up with a mess on your hands as both will be useless. Indeed, this is what you see in many churches that **mix** the Moses' Law with Jesus' grace. People don't know exactly what to believe. Is He the God that makes His people righteous by His Son? Or, is He the God that demands that His people follow the Mosaic Law for their righteousness?

Let's look again at the wineskins. Wineskins carry wine, and wine is also called the "blood of the grape." Wine is used in both the Old and New Covenants to represent blood. The blood of the Old Covenant was the blood of bulls and goats, but the blood of the New Covenant is the precious blood of Jesus. The powerful picture of Jesus' analogy is that when Jesus says not to put new wine into old wineskins, He is essentially saying, "Do not mix the blood of bulls and goats (the Old Covenant) with My blood (the New Covenant)! The blood of bulls and goats is from animals, and is ineffective, but My blood is from God and is totally effective!"

This picture receives additional support when we read what the observers of the Pentecost experience thought of the recipients of the outpouring of the Holy Spirit.

Acts 2:13 – *"Others mocking said, These men are full of new wine"* (KJV).

Indeed, the observers were trying to mock the Believers, but they could not have been more correct. The "new wine" was the spiritual wine of the Holy Spirit. The Believers were having their wineskins refilled with the new wine of the New Covenant, the Holy Spirit, that would empower them to carry out the Father's will and be His witnesses throughout the Earth.

Acts 1:8 – *"But ye shall **receive power**, after that the Holy Ghost is come upon you: and ye shall be witnesses unto me both in*

Jerusalem, and in all Judaea, and in Samaria, and unto the uttermost part of the earth" (KJV, emphasis mine).

The finality of the Old Covenant was so important to Jesus, He again used the picture of the Old Covenant being represented by *old wine* in His final moments on the cross.

Matthew 27:34 – *"They gave him **sour wine** to drink mixed with gall. When he had tasted it, **he would not drink"*** (WEB, emphasis mine).

What is sour wine? Sour wine is old wine! Anyone who knows anything about wine will tell you that when it turns old, it turns vinegary and no longer has any use. It is no good and its time has passed! We can say that its *glory* has passed away. This is the same wording used by Paul about the glory of Moses and the Old Covenant.

2 Corinthians 3:7 – *"But if the **service**[5] **of death, written and engraved on stones**, came with glory, so that the children of Israel could not look steadfastly on the face of Moses for the **glory** of his face; **which was passing away"*** (WEB, emphasis mine).

As I stated at the beginning of the book, some world-wide teachers and pastors attempt to divide the Mosaic Law and teach that the dietary laws and civil laws have been fulfilled, but that the Ten Commandments have not. This next Scripture dispels any doubt as to whether the Ten Commandments should be part of Jesus' fulfilled Law. As you read the Scriptures below, remember that the Ten Commandments were the **only** part of the Mosaic Law that was written and engraved on stones.

2 Corinthians 3:5-9 – *"[5]...God, [6]who has also made us competent, [as] ministers of [the] new covenant; not of letter, but of spirit. For the letter kills, but the Spirit quickens. [7](But if the **ministry of death, in letters, graven in stones**, began with*

---

[5] The word "service," in 2 Corinthians 3:7, is also rendered "ministry" in other translations.

*glory, so that the children of Israel could not fix their eyes on the face of Moses, on account of the glory of his face, [a glory] which is annulled; ⁸how shall not rather the ministry of the Spirit subsist in glory? ⁹**For if the ministry of condemnation** [be] glory, much rather the ministry of righteousness abounds in glory"* (DBY, emphasis mine).

First of all, Paul told the Believers in Corinth what covenant they were competent ministers of—The New Covenant. This is not to say that as born-again Believers we should not be scholarly regarding the Old Covenant, its history, and its pictures of Jesus, as they are abundant. However, we do not minister (meaning to give or to convey something) the Old Covenant, as the days of works-based righteous are over. We are only competent ministers of the grace and truth covenant, the New Covenant of Jesus Christ.

John 1:17 – *"For the law was given by Moses, but grace and truth came by Jesus Christ"* (KJV).

Paul then explained in 2 Corinthians why we are not to be ministers of the Old Covenant by saying that the letter (the Mosaic Law) kills, but the spirit quickens, which means it gives life. Then Paul did something amazing: he singled out the Decalogue, the Ten Commandments, and he renamed it for what it does. He called it *"the ministry of death, in letters, graven in stones,"* and two verses later, *"the ministry of condemnation."*

It is hard to imagine a stronger, or clearer, word picture about the position that the Mosaic Law occupies since its fulfillment by Jesus. So, for Believers, the Law of Moses has no standing in our lives, as our righteousness is in Jesus. For the non-believer, God's righteous standard is still here in the world as a witness to them that they cannot be righteous by their works, so they that have ears to hear will be led to Jesus.

The Strength of Sin

1 Corinthians 15:56 – *"The sting of death is sin; and the strength of sin is the law"* (KJV).

This Scripture bears repeating because of its blatancy and its simplicity:

THE STRENGTH OF SIN IS THE LAW.

In any other situation, or if any other words were used instead of "the Law" people would avoid whatever the "it" was. Bear with me for a moment, as Paul once said, with a little foolishness (2 Corinthians 11:1), as I will be absurd to make this point.

What if the "strength of sin" was wearing shoes? Or, what if riding a bicycle was called the "strength of sin"? Obviously, people who wanted to follow God would then avoid these things like the plague. However, because mankind is conditioned to perform, most readers will gloss over this Scripture like it is not even there. Once you have a grace perspective, it is difficult to read 1 Corinthians 15:56 and still believe that the Mosaic Law should have any place in the spirit-led life of a Believer.

What's more, if you think about it and apply this Scripture to your life, it is saying that the more you try and practice the Mosaic Law, the more strength sin will have in your life, and consequently, the more difficulty you will have in overcoming any sin. Is it any wonder that churches which teach adherence to the Ten Commandments, and preach against a particular sin, many times find that exact sin taking hold in their congregations? We should be preaching about the love, grace and truth of our Messiah, Jesus, and the power of His Holy Spirit living in us, to not only change us, but also the world!

Romans 2:4 – *"Or despiseth thou the riches of his goodness and forbearance and longsuffering; not knowing that the **goodness of God leadeth thee to repentance**?"* (KJV, emphasis mine).

Make no mistake, the Mosaic Law is holy, just, and good (Romans 7:12). It just has no power to make us holy, and just, and good.

For the Believer, the Mosaic Law is like a 3500-year-old relic that is now encased in glass in a museum of the spiritual history of the world. You can absolutely marvel at its purity, simplicity, perfection and holiness. You can look at it from every angle that you wish and be in awe of it. Just be careful not to touch this masterpiece, because if you do, it will take every opportunity it can to bring out sin in you. Then, when you commit the sin, it will condemn you for doing it! Indeed, the Mosaic Law works wrath (Romans 4:15).

Galatians 2:16 – *"Knowing that a man is not justified by the works of the law, but by the faith of Jesus Christ, even we have believed in Jesus Christ, that we might be justified by the faith of Christ, and not by the works of the law; for by works of the law no flesh shall be justified"* (KJV).

Galatians 3:11 – *"...the just shall live by faith"* (KJV).

The just, those saved by the blood of Jesus, live by faith, not by the Mosaic Law. In other words, after you are saved you do not go back to the Mosaic Law to learn how to live or how to walk in your daily life. You get saved by faith and you are to live by faith!

I will say it again: *grace saved you and only grace can keep you!*

DANCE WITH THE ONE THAT BRUNG YA'!

Galatians 3:19 – *"Wherefore then serveth the law? It was added because of transgression, till the seed should come..."* (KJV).

Galatians 3:23-26 – *"23But before faith came, we were kept under the law, shut up unto the faith which should afterwards be revealed. 24Wherefore **the law was our schoolmaster to bring us unto Christ**, that we might be justified by faith. 25But after that faith is come, we are **no longer under a schoolmaster**"* (KJV, emphasis mine).

Two Mountains—Two Covenants

Galatians 4:4-5 – *"⁴But when the fullness of the time came, God sent out his Son, born to a woman, born under the law, ⁵that he might redeem those who were under the law, that we might receive the adoption of children"* (WEB).

One of most powerful pictures that the Apostle Paul ever presented, for eliminating the Mosaic Law from the life of those living in the New Covenant, resides in the verses of Galatians 4:21-31. In these passages, Paul, as he often did, contrasted the two covenants, but this time in symbolic form. In this allegory, he recounted the story of Abraham's two wives, Sarah (the freewoman) and Hagar (the bondwoman), and their respective sons, Isaac and Ishmael (Genesis 15:15–21:10). Here he makes some very dramatic comparisons.

Galatians 4:21-30 – *"²¹Tell me, **ye that desire to be under the law**, do ye not hear the law. ²²For it is written, that Abraham had two sons, the one by a bondmaid, the other by a freewoman. ²³But he who was of the bondwoman was born after the flesh, but he of the freewoman was by promise. ²⁴Which things are an allegory for these are the two covenants; the one from the mount Sinai, which gendereth to bondage, which is Agar⁶. ²⁵For this Agar is mount Sinai in Arabia, and answereth to Jerusalem which now is, and is in bondage with her children. ²⁶But Jerusalem which is above is free, which is the mother of us all. ²⁷for it is written, Rejoice, thou barren that bearest not; break forth and cry, thou that travailest not: for the desolate hath many more children than she which hath a husband. ²⁸Now **we, brethren, as Isaac was, are the children of promise.** ²⁹But as then he that was born after the flesh persecuted him that was born after the Spirit, even so it is now. ³⁰Nevertheless what saith the scripture? **Cast out the bondwoman and her son: for** the son of the bondwoman shall not be heir with the son of the freewoman. ³¹So then, brethren, we are not children of the bondwoman, but of the free"* (KJV, emphasis mine).

---

⁶ Agar is also written Hagar; In Hebrew, the name is known to possibly mean "flight".

First of all, Paul identified to whom he was directing his comments: those who desired to be under the Mosaic Law. He then goes on to set forth and explain his allegory: The Old Covenant and New Covenant are symbolic of Mt Sinai (Hagar the bondwoman and her son, Ishmael), and Mt. Zion (Sarah the freewoman, and her son, Isaac.) This had to hit those Galatians who desired to keep the Mosaic Law like a cold slap in the face.

What readers of the Scripture must be made aware of is how inflammatory this comparison would be to people who were proponents of the Mosaic Law. They knew that Sarah and Hagar were at opposite ends of the spiritual spectrum. Reckoning themselves holy, as faithful proponents of the Mosaic Law, they did not initially understand why Paul's picture associated them with Hagar the bondwoman, and they certainly did not want to be! In their minds, they believed they should be Sarah, since Abraham was married to Sarah, and Moses, from whom the Mosaic Law came, was their descendant. But Paul is making a bold statement: Times have changed, and now there is a new standard of righteousness and holiness—His name is Jesus.

Now, according to Paul, if you are of the Mosaic Law (Mount Sinai), you are represented by Hagar and Ishmael. Hagar was the bondwoman; she was not free. She represents the bondage of a *religious system* of fleshly (carnal/human) effort or works-based performance. Ishmael, as her offspring, was birthed by fleshly (carnal/human) effort. He was the offspring of Hagar (bondage and Law) and consequently represents legalism. The point is, religion always leads to bondage.

Thus, Paul used her as a picture of Mt. Sinai, which brought bondage. To further cement his point, he went on to state that Mount Sinai corresponded with the Jerusalem that existed at the time of his writing, which was under the Mosaic Law.

The New Covenant, and its freedom, is represented by Sarah and Isaac. Sarah was the freewoman; she was not in bondage. Isaac (whose name means "laughter") was the promised child, attained by faith and grace (the essence of the New Covenant) and is associated with Jerusalem from above, Mount Zion.

121

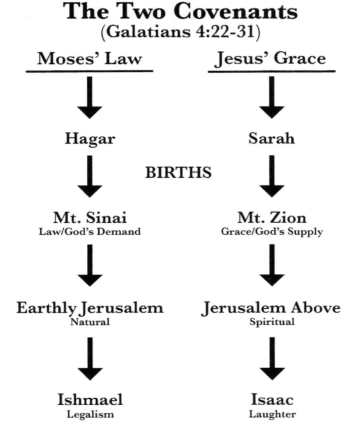

The Two Covenants
(Galatians 4:22-31)

Moses' Law	Jesus' Grace
↓	↓
Hagar	**Sarah**
↓ BIRTHS ↓	
Mt. Sinai Law/God's Demand	**Mt. Zion** Grace/God's Supply
↓	↓
Earthly Jerusalem Natural	**Jerusalem Above** Spiritual
↓	↓
Ishmael Legalism	**Isaac** Laughter

Which one do you desire to live in?

This metaphor of the New Covenant being represented by Mount Zion was confirmed when the writer of Hebrews 12:18-22 contrasted the Old Covenant and Mount Sinai with the New Covenant and Mount Zion.

Hebrews 12:18, 22 – *"¹⁸For you have not come to a mountain that might be touched, and that burned with fire* [Mt. Sinai, the Old Covenant] *..."*

²²But you have come to Mount Zion, and to the city of the living God, the heavenly Jerusalem [the New Covenant] *..."* (WEB, emphasis mine).

In the middle of his allegory, Paul quoted the encouraging prophecy of Isaiah 54:1, referencing the barren and the desolate—Sarah. Paul repeated God's promise from Isaiah's prophecy that the (spiritual) offspring of Sarah would be more than those of Hagar.

Galatians 4:27 – *"For it is written, "Rejoice, you barren who don't bear. Break forth and shout, you that don't travail. For more are the children of the desolate than of her who has a husband"* (WEB).

This is a direct reference to Sarah, who was barren and did not travail (use her own strength), but through the supernatural intervention of the Father she was given power to bring forth the promised child, Isaac, who is a picture of all Believers (Galatians 4:28). Since it was by God's divine promise, God reserved the right to name Abraham and Sarah's son Himself.

God named him Isaac (Hebrew: *Yitzhak*), which means "laughter," or "to rejoice," as Abraham and Sarah had both laughed when He told them they would have a son (Genesis 17:17, Genesis 18:12). They laughed, not in a mocking way as if God could not do it, but because it seemed too wonderful for them in their advanced years. By God naming Isaac "laughter," He effectively said, "I am going to take the laughter you expressed, when I voiced my promise, and mark it forever in your son's name."

For the rest of their lives, they could call to mind their laughter, and the Father's faithful response in the face of it, and never doubt His Word or promises again! I am sure Abraham and Sarah also rejoiced and laughed again, when the blessed event of Isaac's birth took place. Just as God promised Isaac, He has also promised in the prophecy that the sons of Sarah (born-again Believers) would outnumber those of Hagar.

The Apostle Paul then revealed something quite eye-opening. He stated that the behavior, and the typology, of Ishmael in the Genesis story (with Ishmael mocking and persecuting Isaac) would continue, only this time as it related to the two covenants, Mount Sinai (the Mosaic Law) and Mount Zion (New Covenant Grace).

Galatians 4:29 – *"But as then, he who was born according to the flesh persecuted him who was born according to the Spirit, so also it is now"* (WEB).

Paul was saying that just as Ishmael persecuted Isaac (Genesis 21:9), today those who preach adherence to the Mosaic Law and legalism (or the mixing of law and grace) will continue to persecute those who believe in the sufficiency of Jesus' Grace Covenant alone, the Law of the Spirit.

Thankfully, Paul also provided a remedy for dealing with the people, promoting Hagar and Ishmael's Mosaic Law and legalism, when he quoted Sarah's words from Genesis 21:10.

Galatians 4:30-31 – *"³⁰Nevertheless what saith the scripture?* ***Cast out the bondwoman and her son****: for the son of the bondwoman shall not be heir with the son of the freewoman. ³¹So then, brethren, we are not children of the bondwoman, but of the free"* (KJV, emphasis mine).

The above Scriptures are not an excuse to be spiritually immature and call out your pastor or other Believers onto the carpet every time you believe they have uttered something that sounds like legalism or the Mosaic Law. What it should do for you, first, is alert you to you!

First, you need to examine yourself and your own life to see if you currently are under any condemnation of the Mosaic Law or legalism. As a Believer, you may understand that the Mosaic Law has been fulfilled, but have you been deceived into creating laws for yourself? For instance, when you fall short, do you condemn yourself? If you have, unfortunately you have created legalism (Ishmael) in your own life.

For example, have you condemned yourself for vows or promises you have made to a parent or friend that you have not been able to keep? (This is not an excuse for breaking your word, but at times it happens.) Are you freely forgiving people when they offend you, even if they have not expressed remorse and apologized? If you have caused an offense, are you quick to apologize? Do you walk in healthy love, not only with yourself, but the rest of the Body of Christ—your brothers and sisters in the Lord? In short, *have you cast out the bondwoman and her son in your own life?*

Secondly, this scripture should encourage you to examine what you are receiving in your spirit from your pastor. There are some denominations that, as a whole, believe in grace for salvation, but for holiness they still preach adherence to the Mosaic Law and the Ten Commandments. Paul is quite clear that this is not the pure Gospel that he preached.

Also, be advised of a couple of other spiritual points. In the Genesis story, Ishmael did not mock or persecute Isaac until the time of Isaac's weaning or until he could start eating solid food for himself. In other words, the people who advocate mixing law and grace will not persecute you as a grace-only Believer as long as you are a "baby" and need only "spiritual milk." However, when you begin to want to feed yourself on the Word and begin to grow and are *established in righteousness*, this is when their legalism will begin to show.

Hebrews 5:13 – *"For everyone who lives on milk is not experienced in the word of righteousness, for he is a baby"* (WEB).

The last point that I will share is related to Sarah's words, that the son of the bondwoman would not be an heir with Isaac (Genesis 21:10, Galatians 4:30). If you are wanting to fully inherit the grace promises of God, the words Sarah spoke would seem to indicate that as long as Hagar and Ishmael (bondage and legalism) are in residence in your life, you won't be able to fully inherit the grace promises of God.

What we can take away from Paul's allegory of 1) Mount Sinai (Hagar and Ishmael, law) and 2) Mount Zion (Sarah and Isaac, grace), is that Paul is chastising the Galatians who wish to be under the Mosaic Law. By Paul's reckoning, they are not fully of the New Covenant, as they are a picture of the bondage and flesh of the Old Covenant, and not the freedom and spirit of the New Covenant.

As a side note, it is also important to see that religious bondage and legalism can also bring arrogance and deception. You can be under the Mosaic Law, with its bondage and demanded performance, for so long that you cease to recognize that you are even in bondage and will proudly stand on your carnal performance to the Mosaic Law.

John 8:31-33 – *"*[31]*Then said Jesus to those **Jews which believed on him**, If ye continue in my word, then are ye my disciples indeed;* [32]*And ye shall know the truth, and the truth shall make you free.* [33]*They answered him, We be Abraham's seed, and were **never in bondage to any man**: how sayest thou, Ye shall be made free?"* (KJV, emphasis mine).

These were Jews who had believed in Jesus, yet they persisted in holding on to the Mosaic Law. Jesus told them that if they continued in His word, they would know the truth and they would be freed from their bondage and legalism. They, on the other hand, countered Him with pride and arrogance, with an eye toward trumping what Jesus had shared, saying they were Abraham's seed, and had never been in bondage to anyone. Yet, they as a people had been conquered many times, and even then, were under the rule and bondage of the Romans as well as the Mosaic Law.

They ended by questioning how they could be made free, since they thought they already were. Their problem was, they had been in bondage—naturally to conquering forces, and spiritually to the Mosaic Law—for so long, they did not even realize that they were not free!

Believers can also be deceived into thinking, as Hagar and Ishmael were, that something is ours (the inheritance) because of our performance or efforts. It is an attitude that conveys pride, haughtiness, and deservedness. In other words, "I deserve healing because I have prayed for four hours a day for the past four months." The truth is, it is only by Jesus' finished work, and His grace, that we receive anything by faith!

More Anti-Law Evidence

Galatians 5:4 – *"Christ is become of no effect unto you, whosoever of you are justified by the law; ye are fallen from grace"* (KJV).

Philippians 3:7-8 – *"⁷But what things were gain to me, those I counted loss for Christ. ⁸Yea doubtless, and I count all things but loss for the excellency of the knowledge of Christ Jesus my Lord: for whom I have suffered the loss of all things, and do count them but dung, that I may win Christ"* (KJV).

In Philippians 3:5-6, Paul outlined his religious pedigree, citing the fact that he was a "Hebrew of the Hebrews," and concerning the Mosaic Law, a Pharisee. Paul was an absolute expert regarding the Torah. Yet, as he recounted in verses seven and eight, he saw that all his learning of the Torah was just religion and counted it all as **dung.** Yes, Paul, in the American vernacular, called all of his Mosaic Law learning as a Pharisee a pile of you-know-what! And what's more, he stated he did not care about any of his learning as a Pharisee, so that he could gain Christ.

Hebrews 7:18-19 – *"¹⁸For there is an annulling of a foregoing commandment because of its weakness and uselessness ¹⁹(for the law made nothing perfect), and a bringing in of a better hope, through which we draw near to God"* (WEB).

Hebrews 8:7 – *"For if that first covenant had been faultless, then no place would have been sought for a second"* (WEB).

Hebrews 8:13 – *"In that he says, "A new covenant," he has made the first old. But that which is becoming old and grows aged is near to vanishing away"* (WEB).

Hebrews 10:9-10 – *"⁹…He takes away the first, that he may establish the second, ¹⁰by which will we have been sanctified through the offering of the body of Jesus Christ once for all"* (WEB).

The New Covenant Not Like the Old Covenant

Now, we are about to come to a Scripture that if you are a Believer and advocate following the Ten Commandments of the Mosaic Law, you will probably be familiar with, and quote it, as part of your reasoning why the Mosaic Law should be adhered to in the New Covenant. When my wife and I were following the Torah, it was a Scripture that I often used myself. It is Hebrews 10:16, which is a direct quote from Jeremiah 31:33—almost!

We will see that the writer of Hebrews changed one small letter in particular, and by doing so changed the entire meaning of the Scripture. For context we will start at Jeremiah 31:31-33. As you read these Scriptures, keep in mind that when Jesus was asked what the greatest commandment was, he replied, *"You shall love the Lord your God with all your heart, with all your soul, and with all your mind."* Then, on His own, He added a second part and said, *"And you shall love your neighbor as yourself"* (Matthew 22:37-39).

Jeremiah 31:31-33 – *"³¹Behold, the days come, says Yahweh, that I will make a new covenant with the house of Israel, and with the house of Judah: ³²**not according to the covenant that I made with their fathers** in the day that I took them by the hand to bring them out of the land of Egypt; which my covenant they broke, although **I was a husband to them, says Yahweh**. ³³But this is the covenant that I will make with the house of Israel after those days, say Yahweh: I will put my **law** in their inward parts, **and in their heart will I write it;** and I will be their God, and they shall be my people"* (WEB, emphasis mine).

The first point to see is that the Holy Spirit stated the New Covenant would be with the house of Israel and the house of Judah. If you are a Believer, you have an identity with Israel because as a Gentile and wild olive tree, you have been grafted into the natural olive tree, Israel. According to Romans 11:17, we are both partakers of the root, Jesus.

The second point is that upon an initial reading of the text it would seem to suggest that the actual Mosaic Law will be part of the New Covenant, but the Jeremiah Scripture says that this covenant is, "*...not according to the covenant that I made with their fathers.*" So, Jeremiah puts the reader on notice that this New Covenant will be totally different than the Old Covenant. Through Jeremiah, God stated, "*...I will put my **law**...in their heart*"! The Jews that read this Scripture were left with a dilemma. They knew that God's Law was the 613 commands of the Mosaic Law, but how would this be written on a man's heart?

However, when the writer of Hebrews, in the New Covenant, quoted this Scripture from Jeremiah, he made a subtle change.

Hebrews 10:16 – "*This is the covenant that I will make with them after those days, saith the Lord, I will put my **laws** into their **hearts**, and in their minds will I write them*" (KJV, emphasis mine).

So, we should clearly see that the New Covenant, as it relates to the Believer, is about the Believer's heart. This is where the covenant emanates from, because their spirits have been restored to God through the blood of Jesus. Also, consider this: if you know something "by heart," you do not even have to think about it, it is second nature to you. Secondly, you should see that in Hebrews, the writer said that Jesus will put **His laws** in the Believer's heart, not the Law of Moses.

What are the laws of Jesus? They are stated in all three of the synoptic gospels and were initially stated above. In Matthew 22:37, Luke 10:27 and in Mark 12:30-31, Jesus said to love God and to love your neighbor as yourself. This supernatural love is what Jesus said would be the hallmark of recognizing His disciples.

John 13:35 – "*By this shall all men know that ye are my disciples, if ye have love for one another.*"

Why Tempt Ye God

Another very detailed example of why the Mosaic Law has been fulfilled by Jesus and is not for those of faith in His finished work on the cross, is found in Acts 15. Because of the weightiness of this point, we will go into a fair amount of detail regarding this Scripture and its specific wording.

Paul and Barnabas had just returned from planting churches in Asia Minor and were in a city called Antioch, in Syria. Here they were confronted by Jews who wanted to retain the Mosaic Law as part of the New Covenant (Judaizers), telling Paul and Barnabas that unless Believers are circumcised according to the Law of Moses, they could not be saved. Paul and Barnabas disputed this claim, so it was decided that Paul and Barnabas, along with others, should go to Jerusalem to settle the question.

When they arrived in Jerusalem, some of the Pharisees who believed (interestingly, some the Pharisees were also Believers) also said it was necessary for Believers in the New Covenant to be circumcised, and in addition, *"to command them to keep the Law of Moses"* (Acts 15:5). The story continues in the Scriptures below:

Acts 15:7-11 – *"7And when there had been much disputing, Peter rose up, and said unto them, Men and brethren, ye know how that a good while ago God made choice among us, that the Gentiles by my mouth should hear the word of the gospel, and believe. 8And God, which knoweth the hearts, bare them witness, giving them the Holy Ghost, even as he did unto us; 9And put no difference between us and them, **purifying their hearts by faith.** 10Now therefore why tempt[7] ye God, to put a yoke upon the neck of the disciples, which neither our fathers nor we were able to bear? 11But we believe that through the grace of the Lord Jesus Christ **we shall be saved, even as they"** (KJV, emphasis mine).*

---

[7] Different translations of the Bible translate the Greek word *peirazo* as "test," and others as "tempt." According to the HELPS Word-studies of Strong's Concordance, if it is in a positive context it is to be translated "test," and when in a negative context it is to be translated "tempt." Tempting God is obviously a negative, hence the translation should read, "**tempt**."

Peter, the main speaker at the outpouring of the Holy Spirit on Pentecost, and a pillar of the Jerusalem church, was used again here by the Father to render a momentous decision regarding the place of the Mosaic Law in the life of all Believers. He stated that the Mosaic Law should not be a "yoke upon the neck of the disciples." In making his point, Peter described how it was by his own mouth that the Gospel was made known to the Gentiles and that God had also given them the Holy Spirit in the same way as He had the Jews, with the evidence of speaking in tongues.

The weight by which this decision was rendered can be seen in the phrase, "*Now therefore why tempt ye God....?*" As far as Peter was concerned, and speaking under the power of the Holy Spirit, these Believers, sincere as they may have been, by trying to mix Old Covenant Law with New Covenant Grace, *were tempting God.*

If you are scratching your head at this point, you are probably not alone. On the face of it, it seems difficult to understand how what these new Believers were doing was so terrible. After all, practicing the Mosaic Law could only bring about good, right? (Wrong: according to Romans 4:15, it brings about wrath.)

But surely its practice could not be classified as tempting God, when God originated it. They were simply trying to adhere to the Mosaic Law that had been with them for nearly 1500 years. Surely God could not be upset with them for their efforts to continue with His original covenant that was implemented through their great deliverer, Moses, would He? Yes, yes, yes, they saw the value of Jesus and the New Covenant, and being saved by grace through faith, but surely after salvation they were to walk a life of holiness by continuing to adhere to their 1500-year-old Mosaic Covenant, weren't they?

First of all, let us back up for a minute. What exactly does it mean that they were tempting God? In its context, the meaning of the word "tempt" means "to provoke," meaning they were provoking God with their actions. Also, in hermeneutical study (branch of study dealing with interpretation of the Bible), there is a principle called "the Law of First Mention." It states that if you want a clearer interpretation of a word or phrase, you should go back to the first time it was mentioned. At first glance, the first time the word "tempt" is used seems to be in Genesis 22:1.

Genesis 22:1 – *"And it came to pass after these things, that God did tempt Abraham, and said unto him, Abraham: and he said, Behold, here I am"* (KJV).

However, if we refer to James 1:13, we see that the Scripture says, *"Let no man say when he is tempted, I am tempted of God: for God cannot be tempted with evil, neither tempteth he any man"* (emphasis mine). With this in mind, God could not have "tempted" Abraham.

So, we now have grounds to question the King James translation of Genesis 22:1. Whenever we see a verse that does not seem right, we are always well served to go to the Interlinear Bible, which is a word-for-word translation of the Hebrew or Greek text. However, if you are familiar with the Interlinear, you know that it often reads in a stilted manner because of the lack of transitional words. To accommodate for this, a paraphrase of the verse could be rendered as follows:

Genesis 22:1 – *"And it came to pass after these things, that God did **test** Abraham and said unto him, Abraham! And he said Behold..."* (emphasis mine).

So, we see that God did not tempt Abraham. However, He did test him. God did not do this because He was being mean— God is a loving Father. Nor did God test Abraham because God did not know what he would do, as God is all knowing. God tested Abraham so that Abraham would know what Abraham would do, and so that we would have his example.

Since, according to the Interlinear Translation, Genesis 22:1 does not pass the test of being the first time the word "tempt" is used, we must look at the next Scripture where it is used.

Exodus 17:1-2 – *"¹And all the congregation of the children of Israel journeyed from the wilderness of Sin, after their journeys,* *according to the commandment of the LORD, and pitched in Rephadim: and there was no water for the people to drink. 2Wherefore the people did chide with Moses, and said, Give us water that we may drink. And Moses said unto them, Why chide ye with me? Wherefore do ye **tempt the LORD?**"* (KJV, emphasis mine).

This infamous story became known in Hebrew history as the *Massah* (tempted) and *Meribah* (contention) incident. It was such a big event in Israel's history (and God's memory) that it is even mentioned two more times by the Father, through Moses, in Deuteronomy 33:8, and by the Psalmist in Psalm 95:8.

So, how was the nation of Israel tempting God? Yes, they were complaining, but that is not the heart of the matter. Why were they complaining? The issue at the heart of the matter was:

THEY WERE NOT *TRUSTING* GOD!

Even after all of the miracles they had previously seen in Egypt, and how God had later intervened on their behalf against the Egyptian army at the Red Sea, they were still *hard-hearted* as a nation toward the Father. This *hard-heartedness*, or **lack of trust**, is why Scripture records they were tempting God.

Because of the Law of First Mention, we can now review Acts 15 and draw a conclusion about how God felt regarding the people who were trying to mix the Mosaic Law as part of the New Covenant. The verbal comparison on display is that just as Old Covenant Believers were tempting God by not trusting in Him for water, the New Covenant Believers, by trying to add the Law of Moses with the Grace of Jesus, were also tempting God by *not trusting in the sufficiency of Jesus and the New Covenant*. The covenants are not to be mixed. They will not adhere to one another, as one is based on our performance and the other on Jesus' performance. Adding law to grace is like trying to mix oil with water—they just do not mix!

There is also a New Covenant picture of why we should not mix law and grace that is hidden in the story of Ananias and Sapphira, in Acts 5. As we have seen with many of the pictures in Scripture, the names of the people mentioned in Bible stories often tell a separate story and can be quite significant. Such is the case with Ananias and Sapphira. Most Believers are familiar with text of the story. Ananias and Sapphira represented themselves as Believers, however, there is Scriptural evidence that they were not.

The point of the story is that they had held back a portion of the sale price of some property and because they had lied to the Holy Spirit about it, Peter pronounced "judgment" on them both, and they both lost their lives. The picture that we should not mix grace and law is found in their names.

The name Ananias is the Greek form of the Hebrew name *Hananiah*. The meaning of *Hananiah* is "*Yahweh* is gracious." So, we see that *Hananiah* stands for Jesus' Grace Covenant, the New Covenant. On the other hand, the meaning of the name Sapphira comes from the gem of nearly the same name, sapphire, which is a stone. A stone(s) is a picture of the Mosaic Law. So, in this picture, Sapphira represented the Torah, or the Mosaic Law.

What is God trying to say in this story? If you mix the Mosaic Law with Jesus' grace, the result is death! You see, even if you are a Believer in the New Covenant, if you try to live by the ministry of death, the Mosaic Law, it will only bring condemnation into your life. When you allow and accept condemnation over and over, something alive in you will eventually die! Accept it long enough, and it will even shorten your life!

There will be those who, even after all that has been said, will find difficulty moving beyond the Mosaic Law and the Ten Commandments. It may be because of religious tradition, or because of familiarity. They feel more comfortable with the Mosaic Law because they have tried to live by it for so long.

It may seem to them by saying that the Ten Commandments are fulfilled and that the New Covenant is to be lived by grace alone, I am teaching rebellion. Or, they will think that I am extoling grace to the point that people will take what I'm saying as a "license to sin." They believe that without the Ten Commandments, with only Jesus' grace, that there is nothing to hold man accountable, thus we need to cling to the Ten Commandments. However, Jesus knew, and the Holy Spirit revealed through Paul, this simple but powerful truth:

THE HOLY SPIRIT LIVING ON THE
INSIDE
HOLDS US ACCOUNTABLE MORE
EFFECTIVELY THAN THE
TEN COMMANDMENTS ON THE
OUTSIDE!

Paul was not afraid to live by grace alone, even in the face of people publicly accusing him that his teaching on the sufficiency of Jesus would allow sin to propagate. Paul took time to address this accusation in the book of Romans.

Romans 3:8 – *"And not rather, (as we be slanderously reported, and as some affirm that we say,) Let us do evil, that good may come? whose damnation is just"* (KJV).

Romans 6:1-2 – *"¹What shall we say then? Shall we continue in sin, that grace may abound? ²God forbid. How shall we, that are dead to sin, live any longer therein?"* (KJV).

A couple of chapters later, Paul succinctly stated how the Believers are to live their lives of holiness on this earth.

Romans 8:14 – *"For as many as are led by the Spirit of God, they are the sons of God"* (KJV).

When reading Scripture, we should look not only at what is there, but also at what is **not** there. Please notice that there is no mention in the above Scripture about following the Mosaic Law. The way that the sons of God are led is by the Spirit of God. The reason why a mention of the Mosaic Law is missing is that it is unnecessary. If you have God living in you, the internal New Covenant, you do not need an external Old Covenant. This agrees with the Scriptures that state the just shall live by faith. Let's put that last Scripture with a couple of others to prove that the Mosaic Law, including the Ten Commandments, is not for the Believer.

Romans 1:17 – "*...The just shall live by **faith**.*"

Galatians 3:12 – "*The **law is not of faith**...*"

Could Paul make it any clearer? The Mosaic Law and the New Covenant are at opposite ends of the spiritual spectrum. The New Covenant is of faith and the Old Covenant is not of faith.

Paul believed so much in living by grace alone that he stated in Galatians that if someone from his group, or even an angel from Heaven, preached any other gospel other than what he had preached, to **let him be accursed**. To add even more weight to this statement, he repeated it again in the following verse.

Galatians 1:8-9 – "*⁸But though we, or an angel from heaven, preach any other gospel unto you than that which we have preached unto you, let him be accursed. ⁹As we said before, so say I now again, if any man preach any other gospel unto you than that ye have received, let him be accursed*" (KJV).

This is the only place in the New Covenant where a person, in this case Paul, speaks forth and identifies a group and says, "Let them be accursed." You can be sure that the Apostle Paul did not use this wording lightly, but this is what the Holy Spirit impressed upon him to write. This is the strongest wording he could have possibly used regarding what he thought of anyone preaching another gospel or mixing the pure Grace Gospel with the Mosaic Law.

It is my hope that you can see the simple truth that once the heart of man has been changed by the indwelling of God in the form of the Holy Spirit (Galatians 4:6, the Spirit of His Son), and His New Covenant internal law is written on the heart, there is no longer need for any external law(s)—whether they number ten, or six hundred and thirteen. Even if the Mosaic Law was not the ministry of death, would not living by it be redundant? Think about it. If God Himself is living on the inside of you why do you need the Mosaic Law from the outside? This is why Paul differentiated the Law of Moses from the Law of the Spirit.

Romans 8:2 – *"For the law of the Spirit of life in Christ Jesus hath made me free from the law of sin and of death"* (KJV).

What is the law of sin and death? The law of sin and death comes from the ministry of death that we identified earlier in, 2 Corinthians 3:7.

2 Corinthians 3:7 – *"...the ministry of death, in letters, graven in stones..."* (DBY).

The ministry of death is the Ten Commandments. Paul is stating in Romans 8:2 that Christ Jesus has made us (Believers in Him) free from the law of sin and death—the Ten Commandments. First of all, if you, as a Believer, are tired of trying to be Holy, stop looking to the Ten Commandments and the Mosaic Law for your spiritual nourishment and your standard of holiness, as it can only point out your sin and condemn you.

Instead, immerse yourself, and depend on, the love, grace and favor of Jesus and your Father. Only then will you know your true, full freedom in Christ (Ephesians 1:4-13). The Father did not begin a work in you to then abandon you to make you finish His work in your life on your own.

Philippians 1:6 – *"being confident of this very thing, that he who began a good work in you will complete it until the day of Jesus Christ"* (WEB).

Look at the structure of the above sentence. What is the good work in you that He began? The beginning of the good work in you is His salvation by grace. However, after we are saved in our spirits, we still live on this earth, and the completion of His work in us refers to the renewing of our minds in our lives here, and the redemption of our bodies when He returns.

The first important point is that the Holy Spirit is saying that He will complete it—*it will not be completed by your works.* Since the good work in you was started by His grace, it will be finished by His grace. You can have absolute confidence and faith that, if you have given your heart to Him, His Spirit is already working in your life daily, as you yield to Him. It is just that some work is unseen, as it is being done on the inside.

Your friends and co-workers may not see it—you may not even realize it yourself—but it is going on. Just like when a seed is planted, the foundational work is done underground, unseen, but yet it is the most important part of its growth, as its roots will supply nourishment for its entire life.

Secondly, if you are not saved, and your heart's desire is to be righteous and follow God, but you have run from the Father because you knew you could not perform the Mosaic Law, the Gospel is truly Good News, for you! You can now stop running and receive the free gift of God, salvation through Jesus. I can think of no better reason to be born again. And then, as we all must, rely on the grace of God to work out His will in your life. This agrees with what Jesus, Himself, told people to do: to work the works of God.

John 6:28-29 – *"²⁸They said therefore unto him, What shall we do, that we might work the works of God. ²⁹Jesus answered and said unto them, **This is the work of God,** that ye believe on him whom he hath sent"* (emphasis mine).

The Father and Relationship—Not Religion

As you have probably surmised by now, I am a staunch Believer in not only both the grace that the Father has extended to us, along with His faith that He also has given to us (Romans 12:3 & Ephesians 2:8), but also in all the freedom and responsibility that comes along with them. Let me state that again to drive home this point, lest I, as one who is free from the Mosaic Law and in Christ, be called lawless. Just because we are to be without the Mosaic Law, does not make a born-again Believer lawless. Paul said it best when he said that the love of Christ constrained him (2 Corinthians 5:14).

I am sure you have heard the phrase, "with freedom comes responsibility." We, as Jesus' Body on His Earth, can never let our freedom be used as license to sin, and we should never use our freedom in Christ in a way where it will offend someone else, especially any other Believers. Paul alluded to this in 1 Corinthians.

1 Corinthians 6:12 – *"All things are lawful to me, but all things are not profitable; all things are lawful to me, but I – I will not be under authority by any"* (YLT).

Although I believe the Word of God is the foundation for all Believers, and many Scriptures have been quoted in this book, it may surprise you to learn that I am not a Believer in religion, in its traditionally understood sense. Please understand, I do not make that last statement for shock value or to create any type of controversy. However, what I am trying to do by it is drive home the relationship aspect of what Jesus did, as opposed to religion, as this is the key aspect of what makes Jesus' covenant unique and separate from all other belief systems in the world.

Jesus was not trying to establish another *religion*. Jesus, as part of His mission on Earth, was to reveal the heart and desire of God and how He wanted to relate to His creation, man. The way He wanted to relate to him was from His identity as Father. You see, Jesus did not need to reveal God, as God (the Almighty One), to the nation of Israel, because they had had that revelation for nearly 1500 years. Their ancestors had seen His mighty miracles when they left Egypt and His presence at the giving of the Mosaic Law at Sinai.

Indeed, the same could be said for the peoples of the entire world, as nearly all cultures today relate to God as God Almighty, even if they do not know the true God of the Scriptures. Even ancient cultures related to God as "the Great Spirit." However, the identity of God that Jesus came to reveal to the disciples, and to all disciples in the future, was that of **Father**.

We can know this because in John 17:26 Jesus stated, "*...I made your name known to them...*" and He referenced God as His Father in this gospel more than any of the other three. In fact, in the entire Gospel of John, Jesus identified God as Father a whopping 102 times. This is in contrast to the other three gospels, where Jesus mentioned the name Father an average of just thirteen times. Seeing that contrast, we can have a high degree of confidence that "Father" was truly the name Jesus came to reveal in the Gospel of John.

To cap it off, at the end of the chapter, the Scripture below states something quite amazing, that you may miss unless you are looking for it.

John 17:26 – "*I made known to them **your name**, and will make it known; that **the love with which you loved me** may be in them, and I in them.*"

Jesus stated that He made known the name of the Father to the disciples, so that the love with which God had for Jesus might be in them. This is a very pointed reference to the love that the Father has for the Son. There is not a closer or more loving relationship in the entire world than the one between our heavenly Father and His Son, and God wants you to partake of it.

Please, do not miss this truth, as for many people this will be the most important point in this book, and if you will meditate on it, it will really bless you! The Scripture is saying that **the same way the Father loved Jesus, His Son, is the same way the Father loves us.**

Jesus said that, by making the name, Father, known to His disciples, He was establishing for us our own God the Father—

son relationship. He wants us to experience the same type of love that is uniquely characterized by the original Father—Son relationship. The love that the Father has for Jesus is a love that was before the foundation of the world.

Some of you may say, "I thought we had everything that Jesus did for us in our spirits when we are born again." This is scripturally true, but we are all on an individual walk, and until a particular Word, or truth of God, becomes real and alive for us, we typically will not receive its benefit. Often, it is over time that we experience, or appropriate, a particular truth through renewing our minds to the Word.

It is easy for us to see the Father loving Jesus because of His perfection, but because of our own issues, abuses and hurts, and the failings of our own earthly fathers, it can often be difficult to see and experience this same love for ourselves.

A picture that will help us realize and experience this intense love that the Father has for us, individually, is seeing what He was willing to do to get us. Even though the Father loved Jesus with a perfect love, to ensure that we could spend eternity with Him, He offered the Son of His love as a ransom for many (Colossians 1:13 & Mark 10:45). Once we experience the love the Father had for Jesus, we will not only enjoy its benefits ourselves, but we will be endowed with it to pass it on to others. Jesus wants His followers to have and to know the love of the Perfect Father so that we can then impart the love of the Perfect Father to the world.

To add weight to my relationship point above, while Jesus was on Earth, He never suggested that after His departure the disciples should start a new religion called Christianity. If that was His goal, He most certainly could have mentioned it. On the contrary, when Jesus talked about God, especially as I have recounted in the Gospel of John, it was in the context of Father.

Paul later confirmed this when he said that we have been adopted into God's family as sons (Romans 8:15 and Galatians 4:6). Remember, there is no male or female in Christ (Galatians

3:28). We are all identified as sons, because in Biblical times the son was the one who typically inherited.

By His death, Jesus was making a way for us to be restored back to our Father to a position that is even better than that of Adam. Now if we sin we are not separated from God our Father, as we are in Christ as sons and daughters. Further, we have been sealed with His Holy Spirit who is the guarantee of our inheritance (Ephesians 1:13).

Even though we have the offer of this great relationship with Jesus and the Father, make no mistake, a person can make the New Covenant a religion if they believe that Jesus only came to establish another set of rules to follow. That has happened to many people who do not know their son-ship and freedom in Christ. Jesus' New Covenant is not a new bondage/religion. It is a personal relationship with our Father that was not possible before His death. Any performance or works on our part are to be an outgrowth of our relationship with Him and are done by faith in Him.

As I mentioned earlier, the etymology of the word religion is the Latin word *religare*, meaning "to bind." Religion will always bring separation and exclusivity (i.e. superior attitudes saying we can't associate with you because you don't do things exactly as we do) and bondage (i.e. if I don't do (X), God will not be pleased with me and something bad will happen to me). Both of these attitudes are steeped in the Mosaic Law and legalism.

On the other hand, Jesus brings unity and freedom. Jesus said that the world would know that we were His disciples because of our love for one another. You cannot say you love God but hate your brother (1 John 4:20). Never forget that Jesus never pointed His finger at any sinner to tell them they were going to Hell, however, some who say they follow Jesus do this exact thing.

The only people that Jesus was angry with were the religious Pharisees and Sadducees—so much so, that He made a whip and drove them out of His Father's house. The religious were the ones that Jesus warned His followers to beware of.

Luke 12:1 – *"…Beware ye of the leaven of the Pharisees, which is hypocrisy"* (KJV).

Mark 8:15 – *"…beware of the leaven of the Pharisees…"* (KJV).

I invite you to reflect on your own church and how it portrays God and God's relationship to His people and see what character it reflects. Do they portray Him as a God of love, or as a God of wrath toward His people? Is Jesus lifted up in the assembly when they come together? After all, it is the goodness of God that leads to repentance (Romans 2:4).

It is abundantly clear that what Jesus died to give us was the opposite of what is known as religion and bondage. In fact, it was so important that Paul put this point in black and white in the book of Galatians.

Galatians 5:1 – *"It is for freedom that Christ has set us free. Stand firm, then, and do not let yourselves be burdened again by a yoke of slavery"* (NIV).

What Jesus has done for everyone, through His death and resurrection, must be seen and understood in light of all of the other false religions and belief systems of the world. The other religions and belief systems advocate doing one of two things. They are either "self-occupied," where the adherents try to please themselves—in essence, be their own gods (i.e. hedonism, new age religion, mother earth worship etc.)—or they are trying/working to please their god through the works that are prescribed by the doctrines of their particular belief system.

Scripture emphatically states that what Jesus did for us is unique among all these other belief systems of the entire world. Jesus did the "work" for His followers. The followers of Jesus only have to believe in Him, and are acceptable to God because of Him, not because of anything they have done. This makes the New Covenant of Jesus stand alone as unique in the world. All other religions and belief systems demand and take; Jesus supplies and gives.

Because the of the "work of God" on the inside of the Believer, they are no longer striving to please God, as they know they are already pleasing to God because of their position of rest, in Christ. And since a Believer is no longer striving to please God they are now free to be used by God. And when they fall short in their behavior by sinning, they know they have already been forgiven because they live as adopted children in union with the Father through the blood of Jesus.

Revisiting the issue of son-ship: As an interesting point, natural born children are born through blood. We say of children, "They are of my blood." On the other hand, adoption, in the natural, can only take place through legal documents, not blood. Because of this, often adopted children, even though they were chosen, can feel "less than" because they are not of the blood of their adopted family. I find it particularly wonderful that the Father, in His love for us, has made sure that we never have a reason to feel "less than," because in addition to being chosen, we are also adopted through and into His blood, the blood of His Son. Halleluyah!

I began my witness list by saying that since the Torah required two to three witnesses to establish a matter, we should do more and bring forth a dozen witnesses from Scripture to establish that the Mosaic Law has been fulfilled for Believers. Logically, since Jesus is the mediator of a new and better covenant (Hebrews 8:6) we should go further than the Mosaic Law required. In the end, we have brought forth more than two dozen.

Bearing all the previous pages in mind and the numerous pictures showing that the Mosaic Law is not for the Believer, let us finally look at a doctrine that has been taught for hundreds of years that goes against all the teaching of grace and freedom we find in the New Covenant: THE TITHE.

Chapter Six
The Tithe

The entire goal of this book is **freedom** for the Body of Christ. Hopefully, as Scripture says, "*...the truth will make you free*" (John 8:32). With that in mind, my desire is to move you over to a grace mindset in your giving. In other words, let's live (and give) according to the covenant that we are under. To do this, we must move out from religion (bondage)—the Mosaic Law or any legalistic-type giving (even though many may be familiar and comfortable with it)—and over into grace (freedom) giving. If you can forget what you have been taught for a moment, and imagine you are reading your Scriptures for the first time, you will be well on your way to seeing and giving differently: accepting and walking in your position as a New Covenant son, instead of an Old Covenant servant.

I believe that this Mosaic Law mindset, from which tithing was birthed, is what is keeping the Body of Christ from being bountifully blessed in these last days. What is the basis for my making this statement?

Once again, let us look at a picture. All that we are to walk in as the Body of Christ on this earth emanates from Jesus. With our faith (which God has given us) **we are saved by grace**, and that **we have power over sin and the devil by grace**.

Ephesians 2:8 – *"for by grace you have been saved through faith, and that not of yourselves; it is the gift of God"* (WEB).

Romans 6:14 – *"For sin will not have dominion over you. For you are not under law, but under grace"* (WEB).

In addition to these Biblical realities, we have scriptures that show us **we have been healed by His grace**.

Matthew 19:2 – *"Great multitudes followed him, and he healed them there"* (WEB).

Matthew 12:15 – *"...Great multitudes followed him; and he healed them all."*

1 Peter 2:24 – *"who his own self bore our sins in his body on the tree, that we, having died to sins, might live to righteousness; by whose stripes you were healed"* (WEB).

However, when it comes to another topic that Jesus taught on, money and giving, most of the Body of Christ is still not operating under grace, but under the Old Covenant, Mosaic Law of tithing, giving a required ten percent. So, I have a simple question: Does it make sense that the church should flow in Jesus' grace regarding 1) salvation, 2) power over the devil and sin, and 3) physical healing and miracles, but still be under the Mosaic Law of tithing regarding 4) giving and provision?

To begin to understand why tithing is not of grace, remember that the New Covenant did not begin with the gospels. Although your Bible's New Testament begins with the Gospel of Matthew, the inauguration of the New Covenant actually begins at Jesus' resurrection, and then was fully implemented at Pentecost, when the Holy Spirit was given to empower Believers. To confirm this, we consult Hebrews 9:16.

Hebrew 9:16 – *"For where a last will and testament is, there must of necessity be the death of him who made it"* (WEB).

Hebrews is saying that although Jesus was born, walked on this earth, and performed miracles among His natural brothers, the New Covenant did not begin until His death and resurrection. The reason why this fact is important is that we must realize that anything Jesus spoke of referencing tithing during His life was spoken to the specific audience He was addressing, and not to the Holy Spirit-filled Body of Christ that would be birthed at Pentecost. Jesus, Himself, stated that He (at least initially) only came for the *"lost sheep of the house of Israel"* (Matthew 15:24).

This is the reason that Jesus chastised the leaders of Israel for tithing on mint, dill and cumin, yet neglecting the weightier matter of the Mosaic Law (justice, mercy, and faithfulness), but then added they should have done the former without neglecting the latter. He said this because He was speaking to people who were under the Mosaic Law, not because it has any bearing on New Covenant Believers, who are not under the Mosaic Law.

This is the same reason that, when the ruler mentioned in Luke 18:18 asked Him what he must to do to attain eternal life, Jesus quoted five of the Ten Commandments. If Jesus was giving New Covenant truth, He would have simply said, "Believe on me, and you will have everlasting life." Both Jesus **and** the ruler were born under the Mosaic Law. *"...God sent out his Son, born to a woman, born under the law"* (Galatians 4:4). Therefore, since the New Covenant had not yet been fully implemented, Jesus directed him via the covenant currently in force: The Mosaic Law.

The fact is, most people in churches where tithing is preached are giving out of fear. They are fearful of offending God or the pastor because of the incorrect—and many times heavy-handed—way giving is taught. In many churches, giving records are kept that inform the pastor which members of the congregation are tithing, and which are not. This, in turn, is often used as a litmus test for who qualifies to serve in the assembly. Does this create an environment of freedom or does it create one of paranoia? At minimum, church members are giving out of obligation, which is still Old Covenant type giving. They are giving out of obligation or fear, because they have been errantly taught, from various Old Covenant scriptures, that tithing should be part of the New Covenant. But, remember, the Old Covenant has been fulfilled by Jesus and those commands were only valid for the Nation of Israel.

One of the most infamous Scriptures that is regularly—incorrectly—taught is Malachi 3:10. From this Scripture, it is commonly taught that, unless church members tithe, they are robbing God. However, in the New Covenant, Believers (as sons of God) might well respond, "How can I rob my Father of something that He gave me in the first place?" We will address this Scripture and others in detail later.

Let me also quickly add that, in most cases, I do **not** blame pastors, as they are often simply preaching and teaching what they have been taught by their denomination or the previous generation of pastors and teachers. Many pastors, with sincere hearts, are desperately, and in all manner of ways, trying to get their congregations to tithe. However, by doing this, they are effectively shooting themselves in the foot. Why? Well, if you are a member of a church where the pastor is teaching members to tithe, is it likely that you will ever consider giving more than ten percent? Probably not.

This Old Covenant teaching of tithing actually minimizes what members might consider giving, and in the process minimizes what finances come into the church. It also has the added negative result of stepping the Believer away from hearing the Holy Spirit in this area. Tithing fosters a mindset of, "Just pay God off, and you will have fulfilled your obligation to Him." We Believers know that our God is a good Father. Unfortunately, teaching tithing to the New Covenant Body of Christ makes God sound more like a mafioso Godfather rather than God, the Father.

If leaders and pastors would be encouraged to trust more fully in grace, and the working of the Holy Spirit in people, they would release their congregations from the Old Covenant bondage of the tithe. If they did, they would see the same result of grace that they see in other areas. We must ask ourselves the following question: Is grace more powerful than the Mosaic Law, or is the Mosaic Law more powerful than grace?

The reality is, Believers who are being taught tithing are giving according to the ministry of death, and the ministry of condemnation. Because of this, they are not seeing true New Covenant results, because the Old Covenant Mosaic Law, and the tithing that was a part of it, is not the covenant that is in force for the Believer (2 Corinthians 3:7-9).

Please understand, I am not saying that no one has ever seen increase or been blessed from an act of faith in giving a tithe. Scripture does say that the ministry of death (The Old Covenant, Mosaic Law) had glory, but it adds that the ministry of the Spirit (The New Covenant) exceeds much more in glory (2 Corinthians 3:7-9). The issue here is one of truth and an understanding of which covenant you are living under.

Furthermore, does telling people that they are robbing God, as is often taught from Malachi 3:10, and ministering guilt and condemnation to them about giving sound like freedom or religious bondage? I will let you decide.

Galatians 5:1 – *"It is for freedom that Christ has set us free. Stand firm, then, and do not let yourselves be burdened again by a yoke of slavery"* (NIV).

Why the Tithe is Not of Grace

The road we will travel to explain this subject will be in two parts. First, we will review the Old Covenant Scriptures in the Mosaic Law that do, in fact, teach tithing: 1) to God, 2) to the Levites, and 3) to a third group. We will look at them closely and see who the tithe was for, and when it was to be given. (I think you will be quite surprised when you find out the identity of the third group.)

Secondly, we will look at the New Covenant Scriptures that have been incorrectly used to teach tithing and see why they are not relevant to the New Covenant Believer.

From the outset, based on all of the previous chapters, the numerous scriptures and pictures from Scripture, we understand that the Mosaic Law, including the Ten Commandments, *"...written and engraved in stones..."* (2 Corinthians 3:7), has been fulfilled by Jesus. This fact alone would seem to negate the need to explain that tithing, which is part of the Mosaic Law, has also been fulfilled.

However, to be exhaustive in our argument, let's look at another aspect of this point. If a greater command has been fulfilled, then by default, any lesser command has also been fulfilled. Since Jesus fulfilled the weightier commandment of Mosaic circumcision, which was the literal *sign of the covenant* handed down from Abraham (Genesis 17:10-11), then the lesser command, tithing, is also fulfilled. In essence, since there is no Mosaic Law regarding circumcision for the Believer, there is no Mosaic Law regarding tithing for the Believer. These are both true because *there is no Mosaic Law Covenant in force for the Believer as Jesus has fulfilled it!*

Indeed, Paul went so far as to say that if you get circumcised, and you think that this act does anything for you, then *"Christ shall profit you nothing"* (Galatians 5:2), and you are obligated to keep the entire 613 commands of the Mosaic Law.

Galatians 5:2-3 – *"²Behold, I, Paul, tell you that if you receive circumcision, Christ will profit you nothing. ³Yes, I testify again to every man who receives circumcision, that he is a debtor to do the whole law"* (WEB).

Lest there be any doubt as to how strongly Paul was against those people advocating the Mosaic Law of circumcision, in Galatians 5:12, he stated that he wished that those who advocated circumcision would not only circumcise themselves, but *"cut themselves off."* If you have not grasped what Paul was saying, let me continue. The graphic nature of what Paul said is revealed in the Interlinear Bible, where the Greek word for the phrase "cut themselves off" is *apokopto,* which means "to castrate."

Forgive my bluntness in paraphrasing this, but in today's language, Paul was boldly saying, "Hey, if you think circumcision (a partial cutting) does something for you spiritually, then why don't you just go all the way and castrate yourselves—then you will really be spiritual!" Paul did not put up with Judaizers (those who advocated mixing the Mosaic Law with Jesus' grace), and neither should the Body of Christ today.

The logical concluding point is this: if circumcision, a foundational tenet of the Mosaic Law, is not part of the New Covenant, then tithing, a lesser tenet of the Mosaic Law, certainly would not be part of the New Covenant.

However, because the topic is money and giving, tithing seems to have remained a sacred cow that has not gone away, even in the face of all the Scriptures that plainly state that the Mosaic Law, and consequently tithing, has been fulfilled by Jesus.

Let's look at this using some of our old math skills regarding sets and subsets. Let's say you have one item, (A) the Mosaic Law, and a second item, (B) tithing. In this case, tithing is a subset, or contained within, the Mosaic Law. By definition, if the first item (A) the Mosaic Law is fulfilled, then the second item (B) tithing, is also fulfilled. Let me restate, that I am not saying that giving should be minimized or curtailed or that the results of giving are not valid for the New Covenant. It is just that New Covenant giving should emanate from the Holy Spirit in you and not from the Mosaic Law.

The Mosaic Law **A**

B The Tithe

On the contrary, if you can see the grace of Jesus in what I am saying, you will see the following New Covenant truth: If pastors will begin teaching Jesus' grace and freedom in the area of giving, instead of the Mosaic Law, the giving of their church will go through the roof, surpassing the meager ten percent tithe.

Unfortunately, the majority of the Body of Christ has been so indoctrinated into the false teaching of tithing that they cannot see that not only does tithing only belong to the Old Covenant, but amazingly, it is not even taught by any of the writers of the New Covenant after the Body of Christ was birthed at Pentecost.

You read the last sentence correctly: In all of their writings, neither John, nor Peter, nor James, nor Luke, nor Paul, ever did a teaching on tithing. The simple question you must ask yourself is, "Why am I giving?" Are you giving because of an external law of demand from the Old Covenant (Mount Sinai, Hagar and Ishmael), **or** from a heart/spirit that has been restored to the Father, the New Covenant (Mount Zion, Sarah and Isaac)? Are you giving what the Holy Spirit, living inside you, is speaking to you? If you are a proponent of grace, it would seem that there should be only one answer to this question.

Hopefully, this information will be an eye opener for you, because the Old Testament Scriptures referencing tithing that pastors use to teach people to tithe, don't say what those pastors teach they say. The Old Covenant Scriptures are quite plain about who the majority of the tithes were for—the third group mentioned at the beginning of this chapter. You may be surprised by the answer: they were for the PEOPLE.

Ok, you can get up off of the floor now, as I am sure you fell off of your chair after reading that last sentence. Yes, the majority of the tithes in the Old Covenant were for the people of Israel and not for the Levites and priests! With these things in mind, let us turn to the Old Covenant and see what it has to say about tithing.

The Old Covenant Scriptures on Tithing

The first time that the tithe is mentioned in the Old Covenant is in regard to the tithe that was given to God.

Leviticus 27:30-32 – *"³⁰All the tithe of the land, whether of the seed of the land or of the fruit of the trees, is Yahweh's. It is holy to Yahweh. ³¹If a man redeems anything of his tithe, he shall add a fifth part to it. ³²All the tithe of the herds or the flocks, whatever passes under the rod, the tenth shall be holy to Yahweh"* (WEB).

These offerings to God were to be burned up on the altar. It is important to understand this tithe to God was not for the Levites and priests. This is important because many pastors have taken the picture of the tithe dedicated to God and have used it as the reason why members should give to the church. The problem is that this picture does not fit, because the pastor is not, or should not be, in the place of God.

The other picture that pastors have used is that they are a New Covenant picture of the Levites and priests, but this picture does not fit either. The Old Covenant Levites ministered to God in the temple, and the only temple in the New Covenant is the body of the Believers themselves (1 Corinthians 6:19). The only priesthood in the New Covenant is the priesthood of the Believers themselves (1 Peter 2:9). So, going forward I will not be referencing this particular tithe dedicated to God, but the other times when the tithe is mentioned, as it concerns the people and the Levites.

The next time the tithe is mentioned is in the book of Numbers. Here it is referencing the tithe that was to go to the Levites and priests.

Numbers 18:21, 24, & 26 – *"²¹To the children of Levi, behold, I have given all the tithe in Israel for an inheritance, in return for their service which they serve, even the service of the Tent of Meeting... ²⁴For the tithe of the children of Israel, which they offer as a wave offering to Yahweh, I have given to the Levites for an* *inheritance. Therefore I have said to them, 'Among the children of Israel they shall have no inheritance'...* ²⁶*Moreover you shall speak to the Levites, and tell them, 'When you take of the children of Israel the tithe which I have given you from them for your inheritance, then you shall offer up a wave offering of it for Yahweh, a tithe of the tithe'"* (WEB).

Even though it seems that the tithe entirely goes to the Levites, we do not yet have the full picture. To get the complete understanding of the tithe, we must next go to Deuteronomy to find out who the majority of the tithes were for, and why God wanted them brought to Jerusalem.

The name Deuteronomy comes from the Greek word *deutero*, which means "second," and *nomos*, which means "law." In the vernacular, it essentially means "second giving of the Mosaic Law," as much of what had already been stated in Exodus, Leviticus and Numbers is expanded upon in this final book of the Torah. Deuteronomy 12 even begins with the words, *"These are the statues and judgements which ye shall observe to do in the land."* In verses five and six, God talked about where in particular He wanted the Hebrews to give their offerings. Now, hold on to your seats, because the first time I read verse seven I about fell off my chair, as it states who the tithe is for.

Deuteronomy 12:5-6 – *"⁵But to the place which Yahweh your God shall choose out of all your tribes, to put his name there, you shall seek his habitation, and there you shall come. ⁶There you shall bring your **burnt offerings**, your **sacrifices**, your **tithes**, the **wave offering** of your hand, your **vows**, your **freewill offerings**, and the **firstborn of your herd** and of **your flock**"* (WEB, emphasis mine).

Deuteronomy 12:7 – *"There **you shall eat before Yahweh your God**, and you shall rejoice in all that you put your hand to, you and your households, in which Yahweh your God has blessed you"* (WEB, emphasis mine).

In all of the teaching that you have heard about tithing from the pulpit, you probably have never heard that the tithe was to be for the people, have you? And, not only were the tithes (plural, since it pertained to various crops and animals, or it could be worded a tithe of all your increase) to be brought to Jerusalem, but also all of the other offerings of their increase. The people were to gather in Jerusalem, and they were to partake of the increase themselves!

If there was any doubt or confusion about what God meant, He repeated it again in the same chapter in verse seventeen

Deuteronomy 12:17-18 – *"¹⁷You* **may not eat within your gates** *the tithe of your grain, or of your new wine, or of your oil, or the firstborn of your herd or of your flock, nor any of your vows which you vow, nor your freewill offerings, nor the wave offering of your hand; ¹⁸but* **you shall eat them before Yahweh your God** *in the place which Yahweh your God shall choose, you, your son, your daughter, your male servant, your female servant, and the Levite who is within your gates. You shall rejoice before Yahweh your God in all that you put your hand to"* (WEB, emphasis mine).

And again later, in the same chapter, the Father reiterates yet a third time who is to eat the offerings.

Deuteronomy 12:27 – *"You shall offer your burnt offerings, the flesh and the blood, on the altar of Yahweh your God; and the blood of your sacrifices shall be poured out on the altar of Yahweh your God; and* **you shall eat the flesh"** (WEB, emphasis mine).

The next time we see the tithe referenced in Deuteronomy is just a couple of chapters later in Deuteronomy 14. It is here in verse 28 that we get the full explanation of how the Levites were to participate in the tithe that was mentioned in Numbers 18, and more importantly, **when** exactly the Levites were to be given the tithe offering.[8]

---

[8] The priests were also included in this offering since all the priests were descendants of Aaron, who was from the Tribe of Levi.

Deuteronomy 14:22-29 "*²²You shall truly tithe all the increase of your seed, that which comes forth from the field year by year. ²³You shall eat before Yahweh your God, in the place which he shall chose, to cause his name to dwell there, the tithe of your grain, of your new wine, and of your oil, and the firstborn of your herd and of your flock; **that you may learn to fear Yahweh** your God always. ²⁴If the way is too long for you, so that you are not able to carry it, because the place is too far from you, which Yahweh your God shall choose, to set his name there, when Yahweh your God shall bless you; ²⁵then you shall turn it into money, and bind up the money in your hand, and shall go to the place which Yahweh your God shall choose: ²⁶and you shall bestow the money for whatever your soul desires, for cattle, or for sheep, or for wine, or for strong drink, or for whatever your soul asks of you; and you shall eat there before Yahweh your God, and you shall rejoice, you and your household.*

*²⁷The Levite who is within your gates, you shall not forsake him; for he has no inheritance with you. ²⁸At **the end of every three years** you shall bring forth all the tithe of your increase in the same year, and shall **lay it up within your gates**; ²⁹and the Levite, because he has no portion nor inheritance with you, and the foreigner living among you, and the fatherless, and the widow, who are within your gates, shall come, and shall eat and be satisfied; that Yahweh your God may bless you in all the work of your hand which you do*" (emphasis mine).

You may be as surprised as I was to read that in verse 26 it sounds like Israel was instructed to be quite festive, even consuming alcohol if they chose. They, of course, were not to get drunk, but I believe a lot of Christians would be surprised that the Father actually has no prohibition against alcohol.

Some groups contend that the wine that Jesus drank was actually grape juice, but if that is the case, it is difficult to explain why the religious of His day accused Him of being a drunkard (Matthew 11:19).

Further, we see here again, in black and white, that most of the time the tithe did not go to the Levites; it went to the people, that they would learn to fear God. The word "fear," as used here in the Scriptures, is not the same as our English meaning, but more along the lines of "to be in awe of." The Hebrews would learn to fear God, who had so mightily blessed them because He loved them.

Then, in verse 28 we see that the tithe that went to the Levites was only at the end of every three years. For two out of every three years they were to be given to, and enjoyed by, the people. However, since the Levites served in the temple and did not inherit any land to produce crops or animals, *Yahweh* made provision for them by allowing them to receive the tithe once every three years.

Now, if you look again at the last part of verse 28, it sheds light on Malachi 3:10, which is so often incorrectly taught in churches across the world. Regarding the third-year tithe that went to the Levites, verse 28 instructed the people to store it up within their gates. The Hebrew root words here are *yanach*, meaning "to bestow, store, or deposit," and *shaar*, meaning "gate, or entry to a city."

So, Deuteronomy 14:28 is more clearly understood, "to deposit all your tithe within your gates or storehouses." With this reading, its kinship to Malachi 3:10 is easily seen. When Malachi 3:10 says to bring all the tithe into the storehouse, it is **only** referencing the third-year tithe that was to be given to the Levites.

Malachi 3:10 – *"Bring the whole tithe into the storehouse, that there may be food in my house..."* (WEB).

Under the Old Covenant System, the people were to bring the whole tithe into the storehouse for the Levites. But this tithe that was to be brought into the storehouses was only the third-year tithe. In other words, it was not something that the people were to do each week, as is taught in so many churches. This was to be done by the people of Israel once, every three years, for the Levites, because they had no inheritance.

On the other hand, pastors have an inheritance, and it is the same one that you and I possess. Should pastors be taken care of by their flocks? Unequivocally yes! But not via the Mosaic Law from the fulfilled Old Covenant.

2 Corinthians 1:20 – *"For all the promises of God in him are yea, and in him Amen, unto the glory of God by us"* (KJV).

You can now see that when pastors attempt to teach from this Scripture that their members should tithe, they are not teaching it correctly. If their members really took the pastor's teaching to heart, they would close their wallets and purses and not give anything to the church until the third year. That would not be good for the pastor or the Body of Christ, and certainly is not the goal of the new and better covenant that Jesus mediates. The salient point is that pastors should not be reaching back to the fulfilled Old Covenant to teach giving, as Jesus has fulfilled and freed us all from the ministry of death and condemnation (2 Corinthians 3:7-9).

To find further confirmation that the tithe for the Levites was only in the third year we only need to continue reading further in the book of Deuteronomy.

Deuteronomy 26:12 – *"When you have made an end of tithing all the tithe of your increase **in the third year, which is the year of tithing**, then you shall give it to the Levite, to the foreigner, to the fatherless, and to the widow, that they may eat within your gates, and be filled"* (WEB, emphasis mine).

A natural question arising from reading these scriptures would be: "Why did the Father want Israel to bring the tithe, of all the things listed in the Scriptures, to Jerusalem, and eat their tithe there?" Why did God require Israel to bring the tithe to Jerusalem, regardless of where they lived, if He was just going to command them to eat their tithe there once they arrived? For instance, if they lived in Galilee, why did He not just allow them to stay there at their own homes and eat their tithe?

The reason that God wanted the Hebrews to bring their tithe to Jerusalem is specifically because that is where He would choose to place His name, and His presence, via His Shekinah Glory over the Ark. It is further proof that God is always interested in relationship with His people, even under the Old Covenant.

God wanted Israel, whom He had married at Sinai (Ezekiel 16:8), to come to Jerusalem with the tithe of all their increase so they would equate their increase, their blessings, to relationship with Him. They would have the results of His blessing, their tithes, in their hands. In this way, God was showing them that their blessings were not ultimately related to their efforts or their works. The blessings that they carried to His presence were a visual representation of His love for them!

Let me explain this another way: if I give you $50 for you and your spouse, or friend, to have dinner, you certainly would appreciate it. However, if we all go out and eat together and you order the thickest, best rib-eye on the menu, a glass of expensive wine, baked Alaska for dessert, and we sit, have fellowship and commune with one another, and then I pay for it all—it would obviously make a much larger impact on you.

This was the goal of the Father for His people in giving them the tithe and then telling them to bring it to Jerusalem where His presence dwelt! In essence, the Father was personally giving the tithe (His blessing) into the hands of His people and then told all Israel, "Come to Jerusalem, and enjoy yourselves!"

So, surprise, surprise, the Father really is a good, giving, and loving Father—even in the Old Covenant! He is the original giver! He is not the exacting taskmaster of His people that He has been made out to be by people who are in bondage to religion. You can easily recognize them, as they typically walk around with long faces, teaching people that the Father is angry with them. As you can see, even here in the Old Covenant, God was not out to get you! God is out to grow you! And He wants to do this by showing you He is your provider, that you can trust Him, and that He loves you.

The reality is that the Old Covenant Mosaic Law and Scriptures that pastors are teaching from to support tithing are being taught incorrectly. In their fervor to get people to give, they have twisted Old Covenant Scriptures to try and make them say something they simply do not say. The irony for the pastor is that if the members really understood and were in agreement with the Scriptures that they were being taught, albeit incorrectly, giving would not increase as the pastor hopes. Instead, they would give zero for two years, and then ten percent for the third, since that is what the Scripture instructs the people to do. Grace may be being preached from our pulpits for **salvation**, however, when it comes to giving, many times the message sadly defaults to the Mosaic Law of tithing and guilt.

If an increase in giving from the congregation is desired by the pastor, then his first desire must be for blessing the people with the truth of the New Covenant. The preaching of the Mosaic Law regarding giving must be replaced with the truth of grace. The Dispensation of Grace is the covenant that is in force now, not the Mosaic Law. In fact, this pattern of teaching the truth of the Word of God first was the way that the Old Covenant Levites and priesthood were blessed, and this general pattern holds true for New Covenant pastors as well.

The Levites were to teach the truth of the covenant that was in force, the Mosaic Law, to Israel (Deuteronomy 33:10). When Israel obeyed, then the rains would come (Deuteronomy 11:14), the crops would be blessed in abundance, and because of this, the third-year tithe to the Levites would be large. If, however, the Levites did not teach the truth, and perverted the Word of God, the people would then not walk in obedience to the truth, the harvest would reflect this, and the third-year tithe to the Levites would be small.

This is why pastors can have confidence that once the truth of grace is taught regarding giving, the giving in their churches will increase. Giving by grace, and its freedom, is teaching New Covenant truth and *grace and truth* came through Jesus Christ (John 1:17). Tithing is Old Covenant truth. Hearing and taking direction from the Holy Spirit about what to give is the grace and truth of the New Covenant. It is the freedom of Jesus and creates the cheerful giver that God loves (2 Corinthians 9:7).

The New Covenant – Does It Teach Tithing?

Let review again when the New Covenant began.

Hebrews 9:16 – *"For where a testament is, there must also of necessity be the death of the testator"* (KJV).

Considering this Scripture, you can now read and understand the gospels from a different perspective. Since the New Covenant was not enacted until Jesus' death and resurrection, and not fully implemented for Believers until the Holy Spirit was poured out on Pentecost, anything that Jesus said about tithing was directed to the lost sheep of Israel (Matthew 15:24), the Jews, and not the Body of Christ.

As mentioned earlier, when Jesus chastised the leaders of Israel for tithing on mint, dill and cumin, but neglecting the weightier matters of the Mosaic Law (justice, mercy, and faithfulness), and then adds that they should have done the former without neglecting the latter, we know His words were **not** directed to His church. He said this because He was speaking to people under the Mosaic Law, not because it had any bearing on New Covenant Believers, who are not under the Mosaic Law.

To review, this is borne out further when the rich young ruler came and asked Jesus, *"What shall I do that I may inherit eternal life?"* (Mark 10:17). Jesus did not say, "Accept me as Messiah." Rather, He confronted him with the Mosaic Law. Jesus did this because the Mosaic Law was still in force, since He had not yet given His life for sin, to establish the New Covenant.

So, since we are the Body of Christ on Earth, our Brother, Jesus (Hebrews 2:11), has fulfilled the Mosaic Law, and His Spirit now lives in us, we know that we have no need for the external law.

What is even more eye-opening are the answers to all the following questions:

1) Did Paul, the most prolific writer of the New Covenant and foremost expositor of grace, ever teach on tithing? The answer is **no!**

2) Did Peter, James, or John, in any of their writings, ever teach on tithing? The answer is **no!**

3) Did Luke, the writer of the book of Acts (i.e. even when the Church was birthed), ever teach on tithing? Again, the answer is **no!**

In short, none of the writers of the New Covenant ever set forth a tithing teaching for the Body of Christ, the New Covenant Believers. The reason that they did not do any teaching on tithing is because it was understood by all (Spirit-filled and Spirit-led) Believers that tithing, and the Mosaic Law from which it came, were a thing of the past. They occupied no place in, and did not have any application to, the lives of those who were in Christ. If Jesus fulfilled the Mosaic Law, and you are in Him, then the Mosaic Law and tithing have no application to you.

If tithing were to be a relevant teaching of the New Covenant, you would think that among the twenty-three books of the New Covenant that were written after Jesus' death, at least one of the writers would have mentioned it, wouldn't you? But no, the word "tithe" does not drip from the pen of Peter, James, John, or Luke in any of their writings.

And if you believe Paul did **not** write the book of Hebrews (as there are scholars on each side of this issue), we can say that the word "tithe" was also not ever mentioned by the man who wrote most of the New Testament, the Apostle Paul. The word simply never shows up in any of his other writings.

However, to be fair, we need to address what the writer of Hebrews says about the tithe and the context in which he uses it.

We will see it has nothing to do with the New Covenant or behavior of the New Covenant Believers. The writer of the book of Hebrews does use the word tithe in his text; however, it is not because the writer is doing a teaching on tithing, but because he was doing something with a much grander goal, as we will see below. (Going forward, because we are considering the alternative viewpoint—that Paul actually was the writer of Hebrews—his name will be used in the text.)

The Scriptures that are often used to teach tithing as being valid for the New Covenant are largely contained in the seventh chapter of the book of Hebrews. It is here that the story, from Genesis 14, of Abraham meeting Melchizedek is mentioned, and it is these Scriptures that will receive our attention. As with all Scripture context is key, so we will—of necessity—step back and examine the purpose of the book of Hebrews as a whole, and then drill down to see Paul's purpose for writing the verses he wrote in chapter seven.

To explain the grander goal of what Paul was trying to accomplish, we must first state the obvious: this book is written to the Hebrews. These are Jewish people who have an intimate knowledge of the Torah (the Mosaic Law), Jewish history, and all things connected with Judaism and the Jewish way of life. Secondly, as I mentioned above, we need to understand the overall purpose of Hebrews and grasp the overarching theme of this book. In other words, what is the major thought that is being conveyed?

The theme for a large portion of the book of Hebrews is, quite simply, that Jesus is superior to all things! Hebrews speaks of Jesus' superiority to angels, as well as His superiority to Moses, the giver and mediator of the Mosaic Law, as Jesus is his maker. The theme continues, as Hebrews explains that Jesus is superior to all of the Old Covenant sacrifices, as His sacrifice was for all people and for all time. Jesus is also superior to the Mosaic Law, as He is the mediator of His New Covenant, based on better promises. Jesus is superior to the mortal priests of the Aaronic priesthood, since He, as high priest (Hebrew: *cohen gadol*), *"lives forever making intercession for them"* (Hebrews 7:25).

Then, to sum up his argument, in chapter seven of Hebrews, Paul audaciously sets forth to make the case that Jesus is even superior to the Hebrews' father-of-the-faith, Abraham. Once you understand that this is the point of this chapter of Hebrews, then the reason for the appearance of the word "tithe," and the rest of what is said in the chapter, becomes clear.

Use your imagination for a moment and think about the importance of Paul's task. If Paul cannot, through Scripture, somehow prove to the Hebrews that Jesus is greater than Abraham, then in their minds Abraham, a mere man, is still greater than Jesus. As such, Jesus' claim of being One with the Father (John 10:30), and the Lamb of God who takes away the sin of the world, could be impugned by the Jews.

The Jews prideful reliance on their Abrahamic ancestry for their relationship to God can be evidenced in several places in the gospels (Matthew 3:9, Luke 3:8, John 8:39-40). This meant that establishing Jesus' superiority to Abraham was pivotal for Jewish evangelism to take place. Because of God's love and grace for the Hebrews, He used the Apostle Paul, the former Pharisee, to trump the Jews' Abrahamic ancestry argument and offered a separate and powerful Scriptural proof from Genesis that Jesus is, indeed, greater than Abraham.

Because of this proof, the Jews will have no excuse not to believe in Jesus as the Son of God. They, along with all mankind, will be without excuse on the Day of the Lord. On that Day, there will be no denying that Jesus is Messiah, the Son of God.

Again, keep in mind that this is the book to the Hebrews. These are people who knew the Mosaic Law better than any other audience to whom Paul had written. Even if the Hebrews agreed that Jesus had historically lived and later died on a cross, how could anyone convince a Hebrew audience that Jesus was greater than Abraham?

This was the thrust of Hebrews 7—not Paul teaching and affirming Old Testament Mosaic Law tithing, as some have taught. Paul, the former Pharisee (Philippians 3:5), as we will see, accomplished this task, and did so masterfully, through the grace and wisdom of the Holy Spirit.

While closely analyzing the Scriptures that Paul used to demonstrate the truth of his reasoning, we will see the perspective from which he used the word "tithe" and its place within his argument. In the end, it will be obvious that Paul was not teaching tithing as a relevant doctrine for the New Covenant but was simply recounting a story from Genesis that his Hebrew audience could relate to and with which they were very familiar.

Paul began the foundation of his argument in Hebrews 5:5-6. While he contrasted the high priest of the Old Covenant with Jesus, he quoted Psalms 2:7 and Psalms 110:4, as prophetic Scriptures of who the Messiah would be.

Hebrews 5:5-6 – *"⁵So also Christ didn't glorify himself to be made a high priest, but it was he who said to him, 'You are my Son. Today I have become your father.' ⁶As he says also in another place, 'You are a priest forever, after the order of Melchizedek'"* (WEB).

Psalms 2:7 – *"…Thou art my son; this day have I begotten thee"* (KJV).

Psalms 110:4 – *"The LORD [Yahweh] hath sworn, and will not repent, Thou art a priest for ever after the order of Melchizedek"* (KJV).

To drive home the point, Paul then restated the last half of Psalm 110:4, *"Thou art a priest for ever after the order of Melchizedek,"* five more times within three chapters: Hebrews 5:10, 6:20, 7:15, 7:17, and 7:21.

From the Scriptures above, Paul had effectively established to his Hebrew audience that the Messiah would be:

1) God's only begotten Son (i.e. not a servant like Moses, Hebrews 3:5).

2) A priest forever after the order of Melchizedek (i.e. not mortal, like the priests of the ineffective, Old Covenant, Hebrews 7:23).

Paul continued with his proof of Jesus' superiority in Hebrews 7:1-7:8, as he was building to the point that Jesus is superior to their father-of-the-faith, Abraham.

Hebrews 7:1-4 – *"¹For this Melchizedek, king of Salem, priest of God Most High, who met Abraham returning from the slaughter of the kings and blessed him, ²to whom also Abraham divided **a tenth part of all** (being first, by interpretation, king of righteousness, and then also king of Salem, which is king of peace; ³without father, without mother, without genealogy, having neither beginning of days nor end of life, but made like the Son of God), remains a priest continually. ⁴Now consider how great this man was, to whom even Abraham, the patriarch, gave **a tenth out of the best plunder"** (WEB, emphasis mine).

To see exactly what Abraham did in the original story, let us pause here for a moment and go to Genesis 14:16-20.

Genesis 14:16-20 – *"¹⁶He brought back all the goods, and also brought back his relative, Lot, and his goods, and the women also, and the other people. ¹⁷The king of Sodom went out to meet him after his return from the slaughter of Chedorlaomer and the kings who were with him, at the valley of Shaveh (that is, the King's Valley). ¹⁸Melchizedek king of Salem brought out bread and wine: and he was priest of God Most High. ¹⁹He blessed him, and said, 'Blessed be Abram of God Most High, possessor of heaven and earth: ²⁰and blessed be God Most High, who has delivered your enemies into your hand.' **Abram gave him a tenth of all"** (WEB, emphasis mine).

Paul's mission to prove that Jesus is superior to Abraham is now complete. How had he proved this superiority? The Holy

Spirit wisdom of Paul's argument is in its simplicity. After repeatedly driving home the point that Jesus is of the order of Melchizedek, Paul took his Hebrew audience back to the beginning of the Bible; to a story from Genesis they had heard since they were children. Here he recounted the story of Abraham meeting Melchizedek and how Abraham subordinated himself to Melchizedek, giving Him a tenth of his spoil. So, it is now very plain for Paul's Jewish audience to see the logic of his argument.

1) Jesus, Messiah, is of the order of Melchizedek (i.e. they are on the same level).

2) Melchizedek blessed Abraham (the lesser is blessed by the better, Hebrews 7:7).

3) Abraham honored Melchizedek with 10% of his total spoils from his battle. Therefore:

4) Jesus, since He is of the order of Melchizedek, is greater than Abraham!

One-Time, Voluntary Offering

While we are analyzing this story, let's also look at the type of offering that Abraham gave. Abraham gave a *one-time, voluntary, sacrificial offering*. Who else do we know from Scripture that gave this type of offering? Obviously, the answer is our Savior, Jesus. So, although it is widely taught and accepted from this story that Melchizedek is a picture of Jesus (and I agree), it is also easy to see that Abraham, and what he did, was a picture of Jesus and His one-time, voluntary, sacrificial offering.

In addition, despite what some pastors have taught, Abraham is never seen, or spoken of, giving a tithe again. I mention this because some—in their desire to make the Abraham and Melchizedek story a teaching on New Covenant tithing—have taught that Abraham gave ongoing tithes. However, there is no Scripture that ever mentions Abraham giving ongoing tithes, or that would even lead us to assume that he did.

Hebrews 7:6-7 – *"⁶But he whose genealogy is not counted from them has accepted **tithes** from Abraham, and has blessed him who has the promises. ⁷But without any dispute the lesser is blessed by the greater"* (WEB, emphasis mine).

The use of the word "tithes," in Hebrews 7:6, does not refer to ongoing tithes, as in time going forward, but simply references the fact that there were many *different* articles that Abraham had taken from the *four kings* he had defeated, and that he had given a tithe of those articles to Melchizedek, one time. Therefore, it required the use of the plural, tithes, yet did not mean Abraham continued to give a tenth of his increase.

This is borne out by Genesis 14:20, *"Abram gave **a tenth** of all,"* and Hebrews 7:4, *"**a tenth** out of the best spoils."* These Scriptures establish, despite what some have taught—that Abraham gave a tenth of all—it was only from the spoils of his victory, and only one time.

Remember the four kings Abraham defeated? There again is another picture of Abraham as Jesus. Why? Because the number four, in Hebrew thought, often represents the world, as in the four directions (north, south, east and west). Abraham, in overcoming the four heathen kings, can be seen as a picture of Jesus overcoming the world!

The Tithe and the Hidden Testimony

The final point in proving that tithing is not part of the New Covenant addresses the Abrahamic argument. This argument supposes that since that tithing started with Abraham, Believers should continue the practice since Abraham was also in a Grace Covenant.

Looking at the Scriptures in Hebrews 7:5-8, where tithes and tithing are mentioned, we will analyze what is really being said, and why prophetically it is of crucial importance that Abraham's voluntary offering, referenced in verse eight, **must** only be a one-time offering. What hangs in the balance is the proof that Melchizedek, and thereby Jesus, lives forever.

Hebrews 7:5-8 – "*5They indeed of the sons of Levi who receive the priest's office have a commandment to take **tithes** of the people according to the law, that is, of their brothers, though these have come out of the body of Abraham, 6but he whose genealogy is not counted from them has accepted tithes from Abraham, and has blessed him who has the promises. 7But without any dispute the lesser is blessed by the greater. 8**Here** people who die receive tithes, **but there** one receives **tithes of whom it is testified that he lives**"* (WEB, emphasis mine).

Alright, let's slow way down here, as there is a lot that is being said in verse eight that gets lost in all the English translation(s). The translators added several words here that obscure the actual meaning of the original text. Because of that, we will once again be going to the Interlinear Bible to get the correct rendering of verse eight.

Hebrews 7:8 – *"And here indeed, tithes dying men receive; **in that place moreover, being testified** that he lives on"* (Interlinear Bible paraphrase, emphasis mine).

Unbelievably, the entire phrase from the English translations, "one receives tithes of whom" is not even there in the Interlinear Translation. Although it is a subtle detail, the wording makes a huge difference in the meaning of the verse. In addition to the added words, the English translations render the remainder of the verse, *"it is testified that he lives,"* versus, *"**in that place** moreover, being testified that he lives on."* If you only read the English translation, you will miss the entire meaning of the verse regarding **where** the testifying is done, and be left with only the vague Scripture statement, *"it is testified."* This leaves the reader in a no man's land, as it essentially says, *"Somewhere* in Scripture it says that Melchizedek lives."

Alright, let's step back and get the big picture of what is being said. By beginning verse five with *"the sons of Levi…take tithes,"* we know that Paul was referencing the Old Covenant and the Old Covenant priesthood. Then in verse six, by virtue of it reading, *"but **he** whose genealogy is not counted from them,"* (meaning Melchizedek), we know Paul was comparing and contrasting Melchizedek, and by default Jesus and His New Covenant (as they are of the same priestly order), with the Levitical priests.

In verse seven, Paul subtly restated the point that Jesus is superior to Abraham by writing that the lesser, Abraham, is blessed by the better, Melchizedek (i.e. Jesus being of the same order as Melchizedek, makes him better than, and superior to, Abraham). Paul then conveyed an additional point when he got to verse eight. I will restate the two different translations below to go into more detail about the difference in their meaning.

Hebrews 7:8 – *"**Here** people who die receive tithes, but **there** one receives **tithes of whom it is testified** that he lives"* (WEB, emphasis mine).

Although it is the World English Bible that is referenced above, virtually every English translation of this verse is the same. However, when you look at the same verse below, and how it is correctly rendered in the Interlinear Bible, it gives the verse quite a different meaning.

Hebrews 7:8 – *"And here indeed, tithes dying men receive; **in that place moreover**, being testified that he lives on"* (Interlinear Bible paraphrase, emphasis mine).

As mentioned earlier, the difference between the two translations is that the Interlinear Bible states specifically **where the testifying** was being done, which was in **"that place,"** in Genesis. So, Hebrews is telling us to look in Genesis 14, as there is a testimony being given **there** about Melchizedek: that He lives forever. It also reveals who, or what, is doing the testifying. Unfortunately, all the English translations leave out this pivotal detail. Because of this error, the fact that Hebrews 7:8 is referencing Genesis 14:18-20, and that there is a testimony *there* that Melchizedek lives forever, is lost.

170

Now, hang with me, as we are about to discover the answer to why it is important to know *where* the testifying was being done.

To begin with, in Hebrews 7:8, Paul used the comparative language, "***And here*** *tithes, dying men receive,*" and then later, in the same sentence, referencing a different time period, stated, "***in that*** **[other]** ***place moreover****, being testified that he lives on.*" By doing so, he is saying that he is referencing not only two different time periods, but two different covenants. We know this because he was doing a similar comparison in verses five and six comparing Old Covenant and New Covenant priesthoods.

The first phrase, "***And here*** *tithes, dying men receive,*" refers to the time period that the letter to the Hebrews was written (even though the New Covenant was in force, the Temple was still standing), where the mortal, Old Covenant priests (i.e. dying men) were offering ineffective sacrifices day after day.

The second phrase, "*in* ***that place*** *moreover, being testified that he lives on,*" references the Genesis story of Abraham and Melchizedek. Strong's Concordance bears this out, as the latter phrase is rendered, "*in that place,* **on the other hand** *being testified that he lives on,*" meaning not only is it a different time period from what was just stated, but the phrase, "**on the other hand**," indicates that what was being said in the Genesis picture of Abraham and Melchizedek is the opposite of what was stated in the first phrase. This Genesis picture is a picture of grace and is prophetic of the New Covenant to come. It stands in stark contrast with the Old Covenant picture of the dying men (the Mosaic Law, Levitical priests) he had mentioned earlier in the verse.

For easier reading, a modern, conversational paraphrase of verse eight would read, "**And here**, in this Old Covenant, Levitical system that is still going on, mortal priests receive tithes, but on the other hand, in Genesis it was the opposite of the Levitical system. In the Genesis story, where Abraham met Melchizedek, **there is a testimony** that Melchizedek lives forever."

It is understood from the text that just as a contrast was being made between the priests (Levitical vs. Melchizedek and Jesus), there was also a contrast being made between the Old Covenant and New Covenant. It is just that Paul was using the meeting of Abraham and Melchizedek as a picture of the grace of the New Covenant, so do not let that confuse you. We will go into the specifics below.

It is now that we can see the importance of the phrase, "**IN THAT PLACE BEING WITNESSED that he lives**." As I stated, Hebrews 7:8 tells us that someone or something in the Genesis story, when Abraham met Melchizedek, speaks and testifies that Melchizedek lives forever.

At this point, you may also be asking, "Why is it so important that Paul prove that Melchizedek lives forever?" If you are a Gentile Believer you might say to yourself, "Why doesn't Paul go the other way around and simply use the fact that Jesus rose from the dead to prove that Melchizedek lives forever, and leave it at that?"

First of all, Paul himself is an Israelite of the tribe of Benjamin, a Hebrew of Hebrews, and identified himself as a Pharisee (Philippians 3:5), so he had an appreciation for his audience. He loved his people so much, that at one point he stated he would be willing to be "accursed from Christ," if it would help his brethren according to the flesh (Romans 9:3). So, it was vitally important to him, personally, that his brothers, according to the flesh, came to know Christ. Proving that Melchizedek lives forever was a way to do that.

Remember, he was speaking to a Jewish audience and wrote repeatedly in this letter that Jesus was of the order of Melchizedek. If Paul could prove from Genesis that Melchizedek lives forever, he would by default prove that Jesus lives forever and is the "begotten Son" referenced in Psalms 2:7. This was the goal of his writing to the Hebrews. The fact that he used Genesis, the first book of their Hebrew Torah that they hold as authoritative, only adds more weight to his argument.

We have to appreciate that, from a Hebrew-Jewish mindset (with its nearly 1500-year-old Torah-Law tradition), the New Covenant Scriptures, even when taken all together as truth, would pale in strength and weight to the Jews in comparison to the Old Covenant Scriptures they were familiar with and had practiced for so many years. For the Jews, all of the epistles were simply written by contemporary writers, like Paul, of whom the Jews had no initial reason to trust as authoritative.

Their mindsets could have easily been, "You say Jesus rose from the dead and lives forever—so what—neither you nor I were there. Where is your authoritative proof?" If you want to reach a Jewish mind and heart, you must relate to them as Jesus did in Luke 24, and go to the Old Testament. This is exactly what the writer of Hebrews did.

Luke 24:27 – *"Beginning **from Moses and from all the prophets**, he explained to them in all the Scriptures the things concerning himself"* (WEB, emphasis mine).

So, if Paul could accomplish this amazing feat of proving from Genesis that Melchizedek lives forever, it would carry more weight with his Hebrew audience than any New Covenant Scripture, or anyone's personal testimony that Jesus lives forever. It also carried the added benefit of being a strong witnessing tool that the Hebrews could then, in turn, use to witness to their other Jewish brethren.

If you are a student of the Word, you are probably thinking, "But, wait! Don't we already have proof that Melchizedek lives forever? What about Hebrews 7:3?"

Hebrews 7:3 – *"without father, without mother, without genealogy, having neither beginning of days nor end of life, but made like the Son of God), remains a priest continually"* (WEB).

Indeed, this Scripture does state that Melchizedek lives forever. However, there are a couple of problems with accepting Paul's statement as truth if you are a Jew. The first is from a logical standpoint, the argument could be that a statement, taken in and of itself, cannot be its own proof source. In other words, just because I say or write something does not make it true. So, although the Hebrews Scripture above does state that Melchizedek has neither beginning of days nor end of life, it cannot qualify as the *"testifying that he lives on,"* referred to by the same author of verse eight of the same chapter.

The second problem is the Scripture itself. Remember that it states:

Hebrews 7:8 – *"And here indeed, tithes dying men receive;* **in that place moreover, being testified that he lives on"** (Interlinear Bible paraphrase, emphasis mine).

So, the real problem is that, according to the writer of Hebrews, the testimony that Melchizedek lives forever is not in the book of Hebrews at all but resides in just the three verses where Abraham met Melchizedek (Genesis 14:18-20)! Let's look at the verses and see what we find.

Genesis 14:18-20 – *"¹⁸Melchizedek king of Salem brought out bread and wine: and he was priest of God Most High. ¹⁹He blessed him, and said, 'Blessed be Abram of God Most High, possessor of heaven and earth: ²⁰and blessed be God Most High, who has delivered your enemies into your hand.' Abram gave him a tenth of all"* (WEB).

That is it. That is all that is said! So, if at this point, after reading the Scriptures, you are scratching your head, you are probably not alone. Where is the testimony that Hebrews says is there? It may have surprised you to learn that there is nothing overt in the Genesis text itself that states unequivocally that Melchizedek lives forever. Yet, Hebrews 7:8 is quite specific that "the testimony" is there, "in that place," in Genesis 14. So, where is it? Is it possibly in some other Scripture?

You can look all through Scripture, from Genesis to Revelation, and the only other reference to Melchizedek, other than what has already been discounted from Hebrews, is a Scripture we have already seen: Psalm 110:4.

Psalm 110:4 – *"The* LORD *[Yahweh] hath sworn, and will not repent, Thou art a priest for ever after the order of Melchizedek"* (KJV).

This Scripture, although it mentions Melchizedek's name, is not about Melchizedek, but is a prophetic reference to Messiah. It states that Messiah is a priest forever but offers nothing *testifying* that Melchizedek lives forever. So, since Hebrews 7:8 references the Genesis 14 story, let's turn our attention back there.

First of all, typically it is a person who gives testimony, but that is not always the case. An object, or any noun (person, place or thing) can also *testify* of something. For instance, a multi-million-dollar house can testify that someone is wealthy, or a grave maker can testify that someone is dead. But in order for something to testify, it must be a noun. The point is that it does not have to be a person. With that in mind, let us look at Genesis 14:18-20 again.

Genesis 14:18-20 – *"18Melchizedek king of Salem brought out bread and wine: and he was priest of God Most High. 19He blessed him, and said, 'Blessed be Abram of God Most High, possessor of heaven and earth: 20and blessed be God Most High, who has delivered your enemies into your hand.' Abram gave him a tenth of all"* (WEB).

It is clear from reading this passage, that Melchizedek did not testify of Himself, that He lives forever. We also see that Abraham (still called Abram at this point) is mentioned, but again, he does not testify with words of Melchizedek living forever either. In these verses, Heaven and Earth are nouns, but they reference being possessed by God. In the last verse, the noun—enemies—references the four heathen kings. So, they are not testifying about Melchizedek, either.

We could try and make the case that the bread and wine of Melchizedek testify that he lives forever, but they do not fit, because bread and wine were not the items Paul mentioned in Hebrews 7:8, where he stated that it is, "*tithes, dying men receive.*" So, to keep the comparison "apples-to-apples" we must look for the same picture in the second part of the phrase, "*but there being witnessed that he lives.*" You may have already spotted what is testifying, but let's walk through it together from the beginning.

Hebrews 7:8 – "*And here indeed, tithes dying men receive;* **in that place moreover, being testified that he lives on**" (Interlinear Bible paraphrase, emphasis mine).

The key to finding in Genesis 14 who, or what, testifies that Melchizedek lives forever, is realizing that Hebrews is contrasting the Old Covenant and New Covenant. The evidence lies in the two key phrases we've been studying, so let's continue to dissect them further.

We have, in the first part of Hebrews 7:8, the phrase, "*here indeed, tithes dying men receive.*" This is a reference to the Old Covenant in general, and the Old Covenant priests in particular:

1) **Men** (plural)—**who die** (mortals)—receiving **tithes** (plural).

The phrase, "in that place moreover" (Strong's Concordance renders this, "on the other hand") means that Melchizedek and Abraham represent another type of covenant—the New Covenant to come. The covenant they are a picture of operates in an opposite manner of the Levitical one. So, what would be "on the other hand," or **the opposite** of, "dying men receiving ongoing tithes"?

It would be:

2) **One man** (singular)—**who lives forever** (immortal)—receiving **one tithe** (singular).

Hebrews 7:8 – "*And here indeed, tithes dying men receive;* ***in that place moreover, being testified that he lives on***" (Interlinear Bible paraphrase, emphasis mine).

The only noun, and thereby the only witness, left to testify that Melchizedek lives forever is Abraham's one-time voluntary offering—**the tithe.** Abraham's one-time voluntary offering is a picture of Jesus. Abraham, and his actions, are prophetic of Jesus and His one-time voluntary offering on the cross that was to come.

So, not only did Abraham not continue to give ongoing tithes, as some have suggested, but it is specifically because Abraham gave a one-time tithe (a picture of Jesus' one-time, effective sacrifice of the New Covenant vs. the Levitical, ineffective, ongoing sacrifices of the Old Covenant), that **his tithe** (the one-time voluntary offering) **testifies that Melchizedek lives on forever.**

We see here a continuing picture, just as we have seen pictures of Jesus in all other things concerning the Old Covenant that He has fulfilled. We could say that, just as Jesus is the fulfillment of all other things in Old Covenant (the Passover Lamb and a picture of the Mercy Seat of the Ark), He is also a fulfillment of **the tithe**.

Let me stress for a final time that this is not a reason or an excuse not to give. If that is what you think you have heard by reading this book, then you have missed the point entirely. On the contrary, if you are born again and baptized in the Holy Spirit, you have been freed from the bondage of the Mosaic Law and its demands—all of them. Including the ones in letters, engraved in stones—the Ten Commandments—known as the ministry of death (Corinthians 3:7).

Because of this, you have been freed from religion (bondage) unto a living relationship with your Father. We are to follow the voice of the Spirit of His Son in our giving, and as we will see below, His voice is the voice of grace.

New Covenant Giving

Since we have proven that there is not a single tithe teaching in the New Covenant and that (aside from the book of Hebrews) even the very word "tithe" does not appear in any text after Pentecost (when the Holy Spirit was given and the Body of Christ was formed), we must ask the question, "Is there anything about giving written to the Body of Christ? Is there any teaching on New Covenant giving in this grace covenant of Jesus?" Yes, there is! And once again we look to Paul, this time in 2 Corinthians.

Paul gave his direction and encouragement in giving for all Believers in 2 Corinthians 8, and it confirms what has been previously read in this book. New Covenant giving is done by following what the New Covenant itself was founded upon— grace. In this chapter, Paul lifted up the Macedonian Church to the Corinthians. He began in verse one by stating the power in which the Macedonian church was operating.

2 Corinthians 8:1 – *"Moreover, brothers, we make known to you the **grace of God** which has been given in the assemblies of Macedonia"* (WEB, emphasis mine).

In the following verse, he then stated what the effect the power of the **grace of God** was having on the Macedonian Church.

2 Corinthians 8:2 – *"how that in much proof of affliction the abundance of their joy and their deep poverty abounded to the riches of their liberality"* (WEB).

Paul then confirmed that it was by a work of grace from God that the Macedonians have been able to give. He told the Corinthians, in verses six and seven, that he was instructing his fellow worker, Titus, to go to them to complete that same grace of giving in them, as well.

2 Corinthians 8:6-7 – *"⁶So we urged Titus, that as he made a beginning before, so he would also complete in you this **grace.***

*⁷But as you abound in everything, in faith, utterance, knowledge, all earnestness, and in your love to us, see that you also abound in this **grace**"* (WEB, emphasis mine).

This is how giving is to be done in the New Covenant. It is a *grace from God* that is built in us through hearing the voice of the Holy Spirit. In chapter nine, Paul continued to tell the Corinthians that giving is a matter of the heart. If there was ever an opportunity to teach tithing as part of the New Covenant, this was it, yet Paul made no mention of tithing. In verses five through seven, he stated that it is a matter of a person's heart, their personal generosity, and should not be done out of grudging obligation.

2 Corinthians 9:5-7 – *"⁵…that the same might be ready as a matter of generosity, and not of greediness. ⁶Remember this: he who sows sparingly will also reap sparingly. He who sows bountifully will also reap bountifully. ⁷Let each man give according as he has determined **in his heart**; not grudgingly, or under compulsion; for God loves a cheerful giver"* (WEB).

Epilogue

If you come away with anything from this book, I hope you will see that, as a New Covenant Believer, you are not under the Old Covenant Mosaic Law, or its subtle offspring, legalism, in any way. Once God has your heart, your behavior will follow. If you have law or legalism in your life, it is because you are allowing it to be imposed upon you, or you are imposing it upon yourself. Please understand that what Jesus did on the cross freed you from any and all religious bondage. You are to walk freely, every day, with your Father, even in a higher way than Adam did. As one of the sons of God (Galatians 4:6), your spirit is now perfect, because as He is, even so are we in this world (1 John 4:17). You are free!

As I stated earlier, I desire that the Body of Christ be blessed in every way in these last days. The Body of Christ, as a whole, is walking in more truth and more victory than it ever has, since the first century. We understand that we are saved exclusively by grace, and that it is not of works. We understand we have power over our adversary, the devil, exclusively by the grace of Jesus. We hear of miraculous healings of sight and hearing being restored, limbs growing out, and cancers being healed, from across the world; and we know that it is, again, exclusively by the grace of God.

However, in the area of giving, a large portion of the Body of Christ is still under the ministry of death and condemnation, the Mosaic Law of tithing. This last bastion of Old Covenant thinking is not of the grace of the New Covenant and is holding up the Body of Christ from walking in fuller truth and being blessed in these last days. If we want to walk in New Covenant blessings regarding finances, we must teach New Covenant truth and cease from mixing law and grace, by realizing that tithing is not part of the New Covenant.

In other words, let the grace of God work in you, and let it have you yield to the Holy Spirit in you to let your heart be bountiful. Have the desire to give by grace, as this is New Covenant truth. The promise of God, as with all things in the New Covenant, is that your return will be better under this covenant of better promises.

Peace and grace be with you in your walk with your Father!

— Alan Joseph Winkler

About the Author

Alan Winkler was raised on a farm in northeastern Kansas in a Roman Catholic household. As with many people that have been raised in denominational households, traditions that had been handed down from the organized church played a major role in how he related to God.

While growing up on the farm, an accident with a tractor front-end loader left his right foot a half inch shorter than the left. Though extremely painful at the time, God would use what the enemy meant for evil for His own purpose and would bring Alan into His Kingdom eighteen years later.

After graduating from college, Alan worked in Dallas for several years. It was here that he attended a church where a healing evangelist prayed over his foot. The result was that his foot grew out before his very eyes. After seeing the power of God in operation in this small Desoto Texas church, he gave his life to Jesus and became a born-again Christian in 1988. Alan later ministered with the healing ministry of Charles and Frances Hunter and saw the manifestation of many miracles in his time with them.

Years later, back in Dallas, while heading the ushering department at his church, he met his wife, Vicki. They dated for two weeks, were then engaged, and were married within the year. As part of their Bible study, they began studying the Hebrew roots of the Christian faith and the pictures of Yeshua, Jesus, that are in the Old Covenant. After living a Torah-observant lifestyle for ten years, they began to see the error and fruitlessness of attempting to walk under all the demands of the Old Covenant as New Covenant Believers.

In 2009, they began to watch the television ministry of Pastor Joseph Prince, and upon receiving the Word of Grace, both Alan and Vicki turned from mixing the Old and New Covenants and began walking exclusively in the grace of Jesus Christ.

Alan subsequently attended, and graduated from, Andrew Wommack Ministries' Charis Bible College, in Woodland Park, Colorado. He and Vicki have been married for nearly twenty-five years and currently reside in Colorado Springs.

CPSIA information can be obtained
at www.ICGtesting.com
Printed in the USA
JSHW032022160323
38967JS00001B/1